Close to Forever

A Life Well Planned

î

By
Victoria D. Loggins

Close to Forever, A Life Well Planned

ISBN: 978-0-9993545-7-5

Address All Inquiries To:
THE OLD PATHS PUBLICATIONS, Inc.
142 Gold Flume Way
Cleveland, Georgia, U.S.A. 30528

Web: www.theoldpathspublications.com
E-mail: TOP@theoldpathspublications.com

1.0

DEDICATION

I would like to dedicate this book to my brother Brian *Buffy* Dalton. I am thankful that God put you in my life, I love and miss you so very much.

FOREWORD

Alexis and Oliver, the love that was supposed to last forever. They met one summer working at the local ice cream parlor and hit it off instantly. Alex was older than Oliver, so she went off to college, where, after graduating early, Oliver joined her. They knew they were destined to be together and after college they began their life together as husband and wife. This was enough for Alexis but not for Oliver. There were often times when Oliver would bring up his desire to have children, and even though Alexis would agree with him, there was something deep in her that feared the thought of being a parent.

There were two children, Meghan and Robert, brought into their world, but not in the conventional way.

The ties of family that should bind would end up being the ones that would tear this family apart.

Although both Alex and Oliver had high income careers, all the money in the world would not save them as a couple or them as a family.

TABLE OF CONTENTS

Close to Forever, A Life Well Planned

Chapter 1

Who would have thought 30 years had gone by so quickly; who would have thought after 25 years of marriage I would be single and moving back to my hometown? When we said I do, I meant forever, and I guess I thought Oliver did too. Now looking back, I realize his forever was somewhat shorter than mine.

We met the summer I graduated from high school. I was working at the Dairy Dip and Oliver just showed up one day. The next thing I knew he and I were working together almost every day and hanging out on our days off from work. Oliver was a year younger than I, and very much looking forward to his senior year; his turn to rule the school I guess.

I was just excited about going from the small town to the big city for college. School didn't come easy for me, so I had no choice but to work very hard at my classes to get the grades I would need to get into college. There were many nights that I would be up very late working on homework, and especially for extra credit if the teacher would allow it. I knew I wanted a degree in something but had no idea what at that point. I wanted the job with the large corner office and the perks that came with the six-figure income. I envisioned myself driving a foreign car, using valet parking, and getting head of the line cuts no matter what event I was attending.

Oliver knew exactly what he wanted to be. Since day one he had spoken of his love for children and his desire to work with them. Also, his desire to be a father was a very large part of our conversations.

As I left for college that fall, and Oliver began his senior year of high school, we both agreed that dating others would be fine. We were mature enough to realize that we would both be experiencing new things and the pressure of exclusivity would be too much. Oliver dove into his senior year headfirst. He made the varsity football team and was on the debate team as well. Monday through Thursday the football team practiced, and the game was Friday night. Debate club took up a great deal of his time in the mornings before school started, which made our late night/early morning conversations shorter and less frequent. At first I had a tougher time with this than Oliver did. After all, I was on a college campus, not in high school. I was meeting new people, learning to do my own laundry, and getting used to not being awakened every morning by my mom's voice singing the wake-up song to me.

As I began to fit in and make new friends, I realized this was going to be a lot of fun, but a lot of work as well. I studied hard, went to campus tutoring clinics, and settled into making my dream of a six-figure income become a reality. The only real problem was that I still had not declared a major and had no idea what I wanted to do, even at this point.

Oliver and I began to drift apart and I was really too busy to realize it until the day he showed up on campus with his belongings and began moving into the dorm. I stood there like a deer in the headlights as he told me he had graduated midterm so we could go to college together. Not once had he mentioned he was even considering this, but at that moment I was very happy to have him there with me. I showed him around campus, and we began doing everything together again. It was just like we had picked up where we had left off last summer. Oliver was very intelligent and quite a fast learner. He was only a

semester behind me, but after a short amount of time, we were on track to graduate together. Four years had flown by and we had graduated and were getting ready to be married.

Oliver had been offered a wonderful position with the local children's hospital as the rehabilitation director for children with disabilities. To say that Oliver was in his element was an understatement. He was surrounded by children who needed and loved him, and Oliver needed and loved them as well. Every child leaving that hospital had a special place in Oliver's heart. Every day Oliver went to check on the kids and spend some time with them. Many, many times he brought his paperwork home to complete because he had spent too much time with the kids and not enough time behind his desk. Oliver seemed so content with his world and often told me the only thing missing from our life together was our own child.

After graduation, I accepted a position with a new, yet small, retail chain as their buyer. My degree was in fashion and design. I had the desire, but not the talent to make clothes or shoes. I could envision the finished product but could not get through the processing part. Heck, I couldn't even thread a needle. As the retail chain began to grow, my business trips took me away from home, and Oliver, much more than I had expected. However, we agreed we could do this; we were mature adults and realized that building a life took work and dedication. We were strong enough in our marriage that infidelity was never even a thought or concern.

Looking back, maybe it should have been.

Chapter 2

Oliver and I had been married about 8 years when the hospital asked him to become their new CEO. It was quite an accomplishment in such a short time, and I was so proud of my husband for all that he had accomplished. I realized how content I was with my life. We were there; we had the six-figure income, we went to great parties, went on exotic vacations, planned amazing romantic weekends, and traveled as often as our schedules would allow. Both of us loved our careers and each other very much. We had the life I had dreamed of, but not everything was as perfect in Oliver's eyes.

He desperately wanted children, and in the back of my mind, I was beginning to wonder if we would be able to have any. I have to admit that I wasn't as consumed to have children because I figured when, and if, the time was right we would have a family. That's all the thought I gave to it. Oliver often mentioned how much he wanted to play ball with his son or teach his little girl to drive a car. He was so ready to be a father, and as the months and years passed I could see the desire in his eyes. I loved my husband dearly, so after more than 10 years, we decided to go the doctor and see what the issue was, and why we had not yet conceived. We didn't practice any kind of birth control, so we determined that there was a problem with one of us.

When we met with the doctor and the tests were completed, there was no determination of why we could not have a baby. Oliver was fine, I was fine, everything was fine, just no baby. We left the doctor's office and the drive home was a long one. We were only minutes away from the doctor's office, but the drive seemed endless. Oliver looked at me with such sadness in his eyes and apologized to me. When I tried to reassure him that there was no reason to apologize, I found myself apologizing to him for the same thing. When we got home, we walked into our house and Oliver broke down in tears.

The next morning, Oliver woke up with a jerk, sat up in bed and said to me, "Why don't we adopt?" He had seen so many children at the hospital who did not have homes, so why couldn't we give a child a home? Why had we not even thought of this? I wanted very much to share in my husband's new revelation, but something inside me just didn't feel sure about this. I guess I felt that if we were to have a child, I would be the one carrying the baby, watching my belly grow, feeling her or him kick, and eating all the pickles and ice cream I wanted without the guilt. I had accepted the fact that we may never be parents, but I had Oliver and I was very content in my world.

Oliver had made an appointment for us with an attorney who specialized in adoptions. He could barely sit still as the lawyer explained all the details, requirements and the possibilities of not finding a child to welcome into our home. Oliver's face was lit up like a Christmas tree the entire time because all he was truly hearing were the good points. I, however, realized how expensive this would be, and the outcome could still be a no. On the way home, I delicately brought up the cost of this, and, for the first time in our married life, Oliver lost any composure he had and shouted at me like a mad man. We had, of course, argued over the years like all married couples do, but never had he turned to me with such anger in his eyes and venom in his voice. He shouted at me,

"You don't want a child! You don't want us to be parents! And you really don't want me to be a father!"

The shock of his anger and the instant reality that he may be right was almost more than I could take. I didn't know what to say, and I couldn't even form a word at that point. I looked out the window and began to cry. I really wasn't sure why I was even crying; whether it was the truth that deep down inside I wasn't sure about this whole parenting thing, or if it was the fact that I had hurt Oliver with my comments. Maybe I was angry that Oliver had reacted so totally out of character for him and yelled at me with such harshness and anger.

When we arrived at home, Oliver got out of the car, slammed the door, and stomped inside the house. It was rainy and chilly outside, yet I took my time to walk into the house. I was standing there in the entranceway putting my umbrella in the stand when Oliver came down the stairs with an overnight bag in his hand, and a look on his face that I had never seen before. I tried to ask him where he was going but my mouth would not allow the words to come out. I just stared at him as he brushed by me.

Chapter 3

With the slamming of our front door, I broke down and truly cried, with all the pain I had inside me coming out. Until that moment, I had not realized I was in an unhappy marriage. I guess I was so content in outwardly showing the perfect life that I hadn't realized we weren't living it.

I poured myself a hot cup of coffee, cuddled up with a blanket on the couch, and began to evaluate my life. I had a wonderful career that I loved and I had a beautiful home that I was very proud of and most would be envious of. I enjoyed the company of great friends, and I had a husband who I thought loved me regardless if we had children or not. Oliver was supposed to love me. This was the deal when we stood there in front of our friends and family and said our I do's. We made an agreement to love each other until death did we part.

I realized at that point we had not held up our end of the bargain. Neither Oliver nor I had been completely honest with each other. Oliver wanted to be a father, but even after all these years I didn't realize how deeply that desire consumed him. I now realized that my carefree attitude was really my way of denying the fact that deep down I was more afraid of being a mother than anything I could imagine. The responsibility of raising a child was too much for me grasp. What if I screwed the kid up, or what if I was so involved with my work that I didn't put our child first? What if I missed the first step he or she took because a new purse was coming out, or the new shoes of the season were about to hit the runway? Would baby's first word be said to a Nanny?

♥ ♥ ♥ ♥ ♥ ♥ ♥ ♥ ♥ ♥ ♥ ♥

All of these reasons came flooding into my head and I sat there in a mental coma, for I don't know how long, until I realized that night had fallen and I was exhausted. When I woke up, I didn't even pay attention to the fact that Oliver had not called to tell me where he was, or even to let me know that he was okay. I didn't even realize it was Thursday and that I should be at work. I headed for the shower, and then realized that I was so incredibly hungry that my shower would have to wait until after breakfast. I went downstairs to make some coffee and cook some eggs. That's when I realized we hadn't gone to the grocery store and we were out of everything!

I went back upstairs, showered, dressed, and took myself out for breakfast to the little place down the block that Oliver and I had frequented many times over the years. We had never been there for breakfast because we always ate it at home together.

As I sat there eating, I couldn't help but watch a young couple trying to get their little girl to sit down and eat her cereal. I realized that could be Oliver and me. That's when I made the decision that if adoption was the plan for us, I would be willing to try!

I tried calling Oliver on his cell and then at the hospital, but only reached his voicemail. I assumed that he was still very upset with me. I just needed to talk to him and we would work this out. Oliver and I were very good at apologizing to each other. We never stayed angry with each other very long. That was just the way we related. I could look into his blue eyes and whatever I was mad at him about seemed to fade away. The reality of it all was that Oliver and I didn't have that many arguments, or even disagreements.

I was kind of at a loss as to how to proceed since I hadn't spoken to him since the day before. The

awkward feeling that I had in the pit of my stomach was one I was not accustomed to, especially with Oliver. As I was finishing my breakfast and getting ready to leave, I realized I had again lost all track of time. The young family I had been watching was gone and an older man and woman had now moved into the booth that the young family had just occupied.

As I rose to pay the check, my phone rang. My first instinct was to grab the phone and apologize to Oliver. As I started telling him I would try the whole parenting thing, my words stopped when I realized it was my secretary, Kacee, who was calling. In all my years at the design house, I had never been late for work or missed a day. I enjoyed my career so much, I saw no reason to leave any issue unresolved, even for one day; the business could not run without me. Kacee had been my secretary for many years and I could not have asked for anyone better suited for me. She kept my schedule straight, booked my travel arrangements for conventions, shows, and client meetings, and I never had to worry about anything. However, today I had worried her, and Kacee was almost yelling as she asked me where I was and if I were alright. I assured her I was fine, but I would be taking the day off for personal reasons, and she could leave early as well if she chose to. Kacee was a wonderful secretary and our years together had made us good friends, so giving her the rest of the day off signaled that there was a problem. She tried to press me for information, but I assured her I would tell her about it once I had figured it out for myself.

As I hung up with Kacee, I went to the register to pay for my meal but the lady behind the register said that it was already paid for. I looked at her with confusion and a question on my face, but before I could ask any questions she told me that the gentleman who had just left had paid for my meal. The gentleman had told the lady behind the register that he couldn't help but feel for me as I sat there looking so sad and so lost in thought.

I thanked her and asked which way he went so I could go thank him, but she said she only saw him go out the door and did not see which way he went. I headed for the door and then it hit me; it must have been Oliver. I headed for home knowing that he would be there waiting for me to come home.

When I arrived home, Oliver's car was in the drive and I rushed into the house to see him. I stood in the foyer in shock and disbelief as Oliver came walking down the stairs with even more luggage in his hands. He had gathered his laptop, his briefcase, and more of his clothing, and he looked through me as though I were invisible.

Oliver walked into the kitchen and I followed behind him, almost yelling his name. "Oliver, Oliver! Why aren't you answering me?"

When he finally turned around, he had tears in his eyes and his voice quivered as he began to speak. "I'm sorry for not calling you last night," he said. As I started to tell him it was okay, he held his hand up as though he didn't want to hear what I had to say. Oliver was looking at the floor and he would not make eye contact with me. I listened as he began to speak.

"All of my life I have wanted to be a father, and after our appointment with the lawyer and the trip home I realized how selfish I had been. That's why I left last night. It wasn't because of you, it was because of me." Oliver softly spoke my name, "Alexandra, I have loved you for so many years." The instant he said my full name my body went cold. Oliver always called

♥ ♥ ♥ ♥ ♥ ♥ ♥ ♥ ♥ ♥ ♥ ♥ ♥ ♥

me Alex, and that moment was only the second time in our life together that he called me by my full name. I knew whatever was coming next was going to be difficult for him to say and for me to hear. He led me to the den where we sat down, and he began again.

"Alexandra, our careers have taken us on many business trips to many places, and though we tried to travel together when we could, there were many times that we both traveled alone. The difference was that I didn't travel alone many times. About 3 1/2 years ago I met a woman on a flight back from a convention in Washington. She and I sat beside each other, and I don't know which one of us first struck up a conversation. We talked the entire trip back about her husband, her kids, her work, and I spoke about you and me, and how much we wanted kids and looked forward to the future with children in it. After our plane landed, we went to the bar and had a glass of wine and continued our conversation."

"Oliver," I said, "I am not sure I can hear this." I saw this picture coming into focus very clearly.

Oliver looked at me and explained that he had to get this out in the open. "Alexandra, I love you with every fiber of who I am, and you have to know the truth. I can't live with the guilt any longer. After we finished our drinks I walked her to her car, thanked her for the conversation, and shook her hand. I don't know what caused me to hand her my business card, but I did, and she took it. I questioned my actions as I walked back into the airport and waited for the flight that I had to catch to get home. I thought she would probably just throw that card away anyway. But she didn't throw my card away; instead she called me out of the blue after several months, wanting to know if she could get a tour of the hospital and a description of the

21

❤ ❤ ❤ ❤ ❤ ❤ ❤ ❤ ❤ ❤ ❤ ❤

networking and fund-raising policies. Ellen's job was to take hospitals in crisis and turn them around by making them financially stable or recommending they be sold off."

As I sat there listening to Oliver talk about Ellen, I knew that what I was about to hear was even more terrifying than I had imagined. He spoke of her so matter of factly, that she almost belonged in our life. Tears formed in my eyes and spilled out as Oliver continued.

"Ellen arrived at my office," Oliver said, "and I was so excited to show off our skills and works that I got too caught up and invited her to dinner. I knew you would not ask where I was, because you were out of town on business and we had already spoken at lunch. I took Ellen to Italiana Café, which happened to be our favorite Italian restaurant, and we enjoyed a nice bottle of wine and wonderful food. We talked for hours about the hospital and our careers, families, and life. Time passed by so quickly that before we realized it, it was already midnight. I offered to drive her to her hotel and she said she would just grab a taxi. However, I scoffed at her and walked her to my car. After some hesitation, she accepted, and we headed for her hotel.

"Alex, my intent was to drop her off, thank her for the evening, and go home to our bed. I'm not exactly sure where we deviated from my plan though. As we pulled up to the hotel, I walked her into the lobby and had turned to go back to the car when she asked if I would like to have a drink since the lounge was still open. I knew you were on business in New York, so another drink sounded pretty good to me. We ordered two brandies and became engrossed in yet another conversation. I don't remember what we talked

about now, but it was hard to pull myself away from this very comfortable feeling."

Oliver paused as he was seeing the confusion, anger and sadness growing in my eyes. I was having trouble breathing and I really wanted to just get up and run. I couldn't believe that after this many years, he was telling me about what I was sure in my heart was an affair that had been going on for years. I sat there staring at him with my mind reeling from all that I was attempting to process, and nearly got dizzy from all the thoughts swirling in my head. Oliver handed me a glass of water and tried to continue telling me his sordid story. I once again told him that I was not sure how much more of this I could stand to hear. Oliver turned his back to me and began to sob.

When Oliver turned back to face me, the words that came out of his mouth were more than shocking. He reached for my hand, told me how much he loved me, and that he wouldn't change what had happened for anything in the world. Those words slapped my face with such fierceness, that before I realized what I was doing, I had slapped Oliver across the face with all the strength that I had. The physical aggression I had just displayed caught both of us off guard. I stood there trembling, and the noise was so loud that it hurt my ears, but I had no idea that the noise was coming from my own mouth as I stood there screaming at the top of my lungs. I am not sure there were even words coming out, just screaming and crying. Oliver put his arms around me and I tried with all my strength to push him away and at the same time pull him to me. He was the one I fell apart on; he was my rock; he was the man who had vowed to love me. This betrayal went so deep that my emotions were all over the place, and I could not think straight. I felt the room begin to spin and I felt Oliver lift me up. That's all I remember before passing out.

Chapter 4

When I awoke, Oliver was there with a cup of tea and some aspirin. It all seemed like a bad dream, and I thought for a second it was just that, until I saw her standing there. Beside Oliver stood a very pretty little girl with long blonde hair, big green eyes, and a curious look on her face. I imagine that I looked at her with the same curious look, and then, raising my eyes to Oliver, I realized who this child was. She was his! In that very second Oliver's words, "I wouldn't change this for anything," made sense to me. He was finally a father, just not with me. I realized Ellen, the woman who had slept with my husband, was this child's mother.

Oliver began to speak and I held up my hand to him. "I understand Oliver. This is your daughter and she is beautiful. But I don't want to hear any more about your activities with Ellen." I spelled her name out as I stared at this innocent child who looked so much like my husband, and even though she was just a child, a part of me didn't want to see her standing in our home, looking up at my husband, asking her daddy if she could go outside and play. Oliver shook his head yes, and she ran out the door to the back yard to play on the rope swing Oliver had hung the day we had moved into this house.

"Alexandra, when I said I wouldn't change a thing I only meant that I would not give up Meghan for anything. Yes, I would have given anything for you to be her mother and for us to be a family, but I did this all wrong and now I have to make it right by Meghan."

♥ ♥ ♥ ♥ ♥ ♥ ♥ ♥ ♥ ♥ ♥ ♥ ♥

"You did this all wrong? Now you have to make it right by Meghan? What about me? What about making it right by me?"

Oliver asked me to join him outside so we could watch Meghan play. As we walked onto the back patio, Oliver sat down on the bench and motioned for me to sit with him. I stood there looking at him and thinking of all the times we had enjoyed being outside on our patio, sitting on that bench looking up at the stars together. I could not bring myself to sit down beside him on our bench. Instead, I stood there looking at his daughter and glancing at him. As he started to speak, I found myself not really listening or hardly paying attention to what was really going on.

I was transfixed now on this little girl that had come into my life so unexpectedly and so abruptly. I wondered what thoughts were going through her little head as she played in a strange back yard. Wait! Was this a strange back yard? Had she been here before? If yes, how many times? Did she come to see Daddy every time I was away on business? Did Ellen come here too? Had she been in our home? In our bed? Had Oliver made love to her in our house? Did she sit at my bathroom vanity and put on her makeup as I did? Did she borrow anything else of mine besides my husband?

"How long did your affair go on Oliver?" I blurted these words with venom and anger. "How many times did you make love to her? How many times did you tell her you loved her? Were you thinking of me as you were having sex with her?"

The questions came flying out of my mouth faster than Oliver could answer, but I really wasn't sure I wanted the answers. I stood there thinking to

myself, *okay, you've asked. Now ready or not, here they come.*

Oliver lowered his head, and in a softened voice explained, "There was no affair; Ellen and I slept together just the one time. She went back to her husband and I came back to you. We agreed that we would never see each other again because of the terrible thing we had done to you and to Michael, her husband."

"I don't want to hear names! I don't care what her husband's name is!" I spewed at Oliver.

He looked at me with understanding and shame in his eyes. "No, I don't suppose you do," he whispered. "Alex," he softly said, "do you want me to answer your questions or do you need to hate me instead?" Oliver rose and walked toward me. I found my body stiffening with his approaching steps and backed away far enough for him to recognize that touching me was a mistake.

"Okay Oliver, tell me the rest."

Oliver took a breath and just as he was going to speak, both of us were reminded that we were not alone in our back yard. There was a little girl who wanted her daddy to push her in the swing.

"Please come swing me Daddy," she cried out. In an instant Oliver was there pushing his daughter in the swing. "Higher Daddy, higher," she squealed as her laughter rang through the yard.

I stood there watching my husband, knowing that his greatest wish had come true. He was a parent, and I was not. I turned to go back inside, but Meghan asked me, "Alex, where are you going? Don't you want to play outside with me and Daddy?" I looked at that little face, so carefree and honest, and realized that I was not a part of their family.

I told Meghan I would play with them later, but right now I needed to get ready to go on a business trip, so I had to pack my clothes. Oliver knew I didn't have a trip to prepare for and the look on his face was one of understanding and relief. As I brought my suitcase downstairs, Oliver wanted to speak. He wanted to tell me not to go, but instead he picked up my suitcase and took it to the car for me.

Chapter 5

I got in the car and closed the door while Oliver stood there looking at me. I had no idea where I was going to go, but I knew I could not stay there. I pulled the car out of the driveway, turned onto the expressway, and began to drive. I had no destination in mind, just the need to be far away from this situation and all the revelations that had occurred in the last day and a half.

I didn't bother to turn on the radio as I was driving. The silence was a welcome moment of Zen, which was soon interrupted by the sound of my cell phone ringing. I questioned whether or not to answer the phone until I saw that it was Kacee calling. "Hey Kacee," was about all I got out as she barraged me with questions.

"Where are you? Are you coming in tomorrow? What's going on with you? Is Oliver okay?"

"Kacee," I interrupted, "I need you to listen to me. I will be taking a couple of weeks off. Please reschedule any appointments that I have coming up. I know we have a big fashion show coming up, but that's not for another four weeks, so in the meantime take next week off and enjoy some down time." I don't believe I had ever said that in my life and the silence on the phone made me aware that Kacee hadn't heard that either. "Kacee, we have been working for many years to make the merchandising part of this fashion house a success, and now it is just that, so let's enjoy some of the perks that should come with this over the top field we love so much! Take a vacation, and that's an order! Spend time with your kid and drink some wine. I will call you later on in the week."

Kacee refused to hang up, demanding to know what was going on. I told her I would tell her all about it, but for the time being, I was going to the cabin for a couple days, and then where ever the winds took me.

Kacee said, "I don't really understand what that means, but you'd better call me at the end of the week, or I swear I will send out a search party for you!" I promised her that I would call, and we hung up.

I truly didn't have a destination in mind, but I did tell Kacee that I would be at the cabin, so that must be where I was to go. The drive up to the cabin took about 3 hours and in that time my brain had begun to process all that had recently happened to my perfect world.

I pulled up to the local country store and as I was getting out of the car, Mr. Statum yelled, "Hey Alex, how are ya? Where is Oliver? Coming up later huh? Good to see ya Alex!" In all the years we had owned this cabin, Mr. Statum had been our neighbor and watched over things for us, but I just realized that I had never had a conversation with him. He was more the rhetorical type, and he asked questions not really expecting or even waiting for an answer. I smiled and waved to acknowledge he had spoken and continued my way into the store. I rounded up some things that I would need and headed to the checkout counter. I put my wine on the belt and the lady behind the register asked for my ID. I couldn't help but giggle a little and promised her I was well over 21. She informed me that if I didn't have my ID with me, I could go to the car and get it or she would be happy to

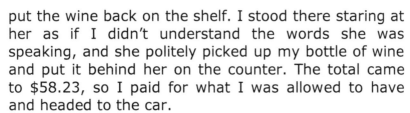

put the wine back on the shelf. I stood there staring at her as if I didn't understand the words she was speaking, and she politely picked up my bottle of wine and put it behind her on the counter. The total came to $58.23, so I paid for what I was allowed to have and headed to the car.

As I was fumbling with my keys to get my car unlocked, a tall, gray headed man, came up to me and said, "You owe me $18.00 for the wine."

I got my door unlocked, threw my groceries in the car and whirled around telling him, "I don't owe you anything; I didn't ask you to buy my wine, and furthermore..."

"And furthermore," he interjected with a huge smile, "I was just giving you a hard time hon. No, you didn't ask me, and no, I didn't have to, but here is your wine. Enjoy!"

As I removed the bottle of wine from his hand my head was racing. What just happened? Did I just yell at a complete stranger for being nice to me?

What should I say to him, I thought, as he winked at me and turned around to leave. "Wait!" I shouted after him.

He turned with a bit of a surprise. "Yes?" he asked.

I tried not to stumble over my words as they came out. "Look, I am so sorry. I am having probably the worst day of my life today and I apologize for yelling at you like a mad woman. You see...my husband..." and as the tears began to flow, this stranger stepped towards me, put his hand on my shoulder and said to me, "Life has its struggles, but we survive and continue on. You will too. You never know where your path will lead." With a warm smile on his face, he turned and walked to his pickup and drove away.

I stood there as his words circled in my head. *Life is a struggle, but we survive and continue on.* I knew I had heard those words before, but at that moment I could not remember where or from whom. I don't know how long I stood there, as my mind was cloudy and things just seemed to be moving in slow motion. I don't remember getting into my car or driving to the cabin, yet there I was in the driveway.

I finally woke up from my haze, got out of the car, walked up the stairs and unlocked the cabin door. It had been quite some time since we had been here, and the smell of cedar and leather hit my senses quickly. I opened the windows to allow some fresh air to come in and headed back to the car for the groceries and my wine. With the groceries put away and a glass of red wine in my hand, I headed out to the back deck that overlooked the lake. Our lake. That's what Oliver and I called this perfect picture of tranquility that we had enjoyed for so many years.

As I sat there as the sun began to set, watching the waves ripple to the shore and the ducks swim, I realized that so many things were going to change in my life. *My perfect life*, I thought to myself, *some kind of cruel twist my life had taken.* The man that I had loved for so long was now a father to a beautiful little girl that was not my little girl. The house that we had made into our home, the friends we had spent so much time with, was all changing now, and I wasn't sure how to begin to keep up with the changes.

I sat on the deck for a long time absorbing the peace and quiet and feeling the warm day begin to become a cool night. It was time to go inside and settle in for the evening. The cool evening air made

me focus on the fireplace that needed to be popping and cracking by now. I got the kindling out of the box and got my fire started. I loved the sounds and the smells of the different types of wood burning in a fire, and as the cabin began to warm up, I went to the kitchen to find something for my dinner. Oliver and I had designed this kitchen. We had overseen every aspect of the renovations, and as I stared at the original stove standing there I couldn't help but bust out laughing. Just like my life, everything in this kitchen had been changed except for the stove, and I was the stove. I guess I find humor in the strangest things, because as I was cooking dinner, I continued to laugh and even sing. If someone had been watching me they would have thought I had lost my mind.

I was almost finished with the pasta when a knock on the door startled me. I certainly wasn't expecting anyone. No one except for Kacee knew where I was. I set the pasta to simmer and went to the door. I looked through the glass to see the man from the county store standing there. I opened the door, not really sure what to say. "Hi," I said, although it came out more of a question than a statement.

"Hi," he said with a wide smile on his face. "I see you got here safely. Whatever you're cooking smells good."

"Uh, yes I did, and thank you." I stood there in the doorway not sure if I should invite him in or just close the door in this stalker's face.

He reached in his coat pocket and pulled out my checkbook. "How did you get this?" I asked. "You left before I did. I watched you drive off."

"Oh, you watched me?" the stranger asked with a growing smile on his face.

"Yes, I did. Well, I wasn't staring or anything. I just...anyway how did you get my checkbook?" I asked.

He laughed and said he had forgotten to pick up the newspaper when he saw me at the store. "Funny," he said, "that was the one thing I went for." Laughingly, he said, "Guess that's what happens when you get old like me. Anyway, I pulled back into the lot and saw something lying on the ground. I went to see what it was, and since I pretty much know everyone up here and I hadn't seen you before, I figured it must belong to you. I called the number on the checks and your husband gave me the address to your place.

"You did what?" I yelled at him. You called my husband? Have you lost your mind! Now he knows where I am. I didn't want anyone to know, and you went and took it upon yourself to call my husband! Couldn't you have just turned it into the store manager? I would have noticed it was missing and I would have retraced my steps. I would have..." He held his hand up to get me to stop speaking. "You know Alexandra, this is the second time today you have yelled at me for doing something nice for you. I don't even know you and yet I find you to be extremely difficult at times. Good bye Alexandra. Have a nice evening." He started down the stairs.

I stood there with my mouth open, shocked at what I had said to this man yet again. "Hey...um, I don't know your name. Can you wait? Can you..."

He turned and said, "My name is Colton, but everyone calls me Colt."

"Colt," I said, "I am not even sure how to keep apologizing to you. Would you like to come in and have dinner with me? I make a great chicken pasta bake."

"Is it safe?" he asked with a smile on his face."

"Probably not," I answered with a grin on my face.

"Then I accept," he said as he began to climb the stairs.

"Red wine okay?" I asked. "Glasses are over there on the rack. Grab you one and refill mine, if you don't mind."

Colt poured his glass, refilled mine, and began to set the table for us. I fixed our plates, carried them to the table, sat down, and as we started to eat Colt looked at me and asked, "So how's your day going?"

I just about choked on my pasta as I started laughing. "Well, to be honest, I have had better!" I looked at him and said, "You are so lucky you aren't wearing my food right now!"

Colt busted out laughing. "Yeah, I was a little worried where that was going to go." His smile made me laugh even harder and I had to stop and catch my breath.

"So Colt, do you normally go around saving damsels in distress? What's your story?" I asked him.

"Well," he said, "There's not really much to tell. I own a place on the other side of the lake. I spend a lot of my time working with my animals: cows, horses, and that kind of stuff. I go fishing every chance I get, and I am wholeheartedly in love with the most beautiful woman I ever laid eyes on. I am fortunate enough that she saw through all the set in my ways, I am right, stubborn ways of mine, to love and marry me anyway."

"That sounds like a complete and fulfilling life you have. That is a blessing Colt, and you should consider yourself very lucky!"

"I do." He smiled and took a drink of his wine.

"I have to ask, won't your wife be upset when you tell her you had dinner in a strange woman's cabin? Oh, and by strange, I mean someone you don't know, not someone who is crazy weird. Wait, scratch that! Both of those words define me pretty well right now, don't they?"

Colt smiled and said, "I am not going to comment on that strange thing!" We both laughed and ate some of our dinner. "This is really good," he said. "You didn't lie when you said you made a great chicken pasta bake, did ya?"

"I try not to make it a habit to lie to anyone, unlike my husband, who seems to find it quite easy."

Colt leaned in and said, "If and when you want to talk, I will be here to listen." I couldn't help but smile and feel that he was very sincere in his offer. I took a sip of wine and asked him again about his wife.

"Her name is Cassandra, and she has eyes that are as blue as the lake, and a heart that is twice as big. We were married for 34 years last July," and that's when Colt's eyes began to fill with tears. "You see, Cassie had been diagnosed with leukemia and we were determined to beat it and continue our lives together. I kept my end of the deal and she tried as best she could to keep her end, but she was just too weak. The disease had taken its toll on her and the chemo was just as hard. She just couldn't take any more. She looked me in the eyes the night she passed and told me it was time for her to go and that I would be okay. She told me to remember always that she loved me and would not trade one moment of our life together."

Colt cleared his throat and said, "My Cassie was a strong-willed woman. Once we disagreed on the color of the barn. She said it had to be pink, and I

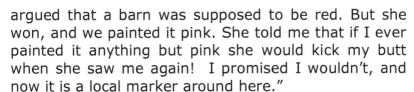

argued that a barn was supposed to be red. But she won, and we painted it pink. She told me that if I ever painted it anything but pink she would kick my butt when she saw me again! I promised I wouldn't, and now it is a local marker around here."

Colt gave a small giggle. "Who paints a barn pink?" he asked. "Anyway, I held her in my arms and as she took her last breath, I told her how much I loved her."

With that, Colt stood up and started clearing the dishes. I sat there lost in his story and wondering how I would feel if Oliver were here with me right now. I loved my husband very much, but right now I was too angry and hurt to continue thinking about anything that had to do with him. I slowly stood up, followed Colt to the kitchen, and asked if he wanted some coffee.

Colt turned to me and said, "So that's my story. What's yours?"

I laughed and said, "Let's save that for another time, can we?"

Colt shook his head in agreement and we put the dishes in the dishwasher and cleaned the kitchen up together. Colt said it was getting late and he was heading back across the lake, but the next dinner was on him. As he headed out to leave I thanked him for sharing his story with me and for the company that I didn't realize I needed.

He looked at me and said, "Life has its struggles, but we survive...and continue on." I smiled and closed the door behind him.

Chapter 6

I was tired and ready for a hot bath. As I ran the bath water, my thought was that I should call Oliver and tell him about this wonderful man I had met and how much he would like Colt. I am sure Oliver was waiting to hear from me; I guess I am sure he was waiting to hear from me. I am sure of only one thing at this moment, and that is that a hot bath is calling my name. I spent about an hour in the tub, reading an old book I had left here last time we had come up. I had forgotten how much I loved to read. I got so engrossed in the book that the water cooling down was my signal to get out. I put on my night clothes, stoked the fire and turned in for the night. The moon was so bright through the skylight that I counted stars and fell into a sound sleep.

I woke up the next morning and realized I didn't even know what day it was. I had been in such a fog for the last few days, I was unaware that it was already Monday morning. I knew I had given Kacee the week off, more like demanded she take the week off, but I knew that when I called she would answer the phone. I picked up the phone and called my office and like clockwork Kacee's voice was what I heard instead of the answering service.

"Kacee, what are you doing there? I told you take the week off and enjoy some down time!"

"Alex!" she yelled, "Are you okay? You said you would call, but you didn't. I tried calling you, and I left several voice messages for you. Why haven't you called me back until now?"

"Kacee, slow down. I am fine. I'm sorry I haven't called you back until now, but I had to start to clear my head. I'm still at the cabin and I am going to take this week to sort some things out and..."

Kacee interrupted, "Sort what things out? Why aren't you talking to me Alex? I miss you, and Oliver has called asking if I have heard from you. What happened?"

"Okay Kacee, this is how this is going to work. "You finish whatever you are doing, go home and call me tonight. I promise to answer the phone when you call. Now get out of that office and take the rest of the week off! I will talk to you later."

"Promise?" Kacee asked.

"I promise," I said and hung up the phone. I decided to stay here for a couple of weeks. I could work from here, clear my head, and enjoy the lake. I decided to go for a walk around the lake and take in the beauty of this area. I was about half way around when I noticed a pink barn. It was a ways off, but how do you not notice a pink barn? I couldn't help but smile and reminisce about the dinner company I had last night.

After my walk, I got into the car and headed for the pink barn. As many times as Oliver and I had come up for the weekend and vacations, I was still very unfamiliar with all the roads. I knew I must be heading in the right direction as the pink barn was getting closer to me. I turned down the road to the right which was named Cassandra Lane. I was pretty sure at that point that I was on the right road. I drove for what seemed like ten miles to find a mansion of a brick home with a pink barn in the far back yard. The way Colt had described this place when he said, "I own a place on the other side of the lake," was an understatement. This was a ranch, and a beautiful one at that!

♥ ♥ ♥ ♥ ♥ ♥ ♥ ♥ ♥ ♥ ♥ ♥ ♥

I put the car in park and turned the engine off, getting ready to get out when I heard, "Watch where you step; we just brought the horses through." I saw a big smile on Colt's face as he was pointing to the gifts the horses had left on the ground right where I was going to step.

"Thanks for the warning," I shouted, "These are my good tennis shoes." We both laughed as Colt came walking up taking off his work gloves.

"What brings you out here to my little place across the lake? It's not dinner time yet, although I could use some breakfast, come to think of it," Colt said with a grin on his face. I couldn't help but grin back at him.

"I wanted to thank you again for a lovely evening yesterday and sharing your world with me. Oh yeah, little place? This is beautiful but there is nothing little about this...anywhere!! Your home is breathtaking and the pink barn, I totally understand Cassandra's thought process with it! How small is your ranch?"

Colt looked at me and laughed. "We have about 500 acres, give or take a few."

"A few? A few what? Hundred? No, really Colt, this is amazing. I am sure your wife loved it here."

"Yes she did Alex, and I was fortunate enough to give her the life she deserved to have. I have to admit though, it wasn't my brilliant brain that got us here. It was family land and it was handed down to me. My grandfather was big in the cattle business and made a lot of very wise investments. I am very fortunate as I didn't care much for school. Now don't get me wrong, I believe in all the book learning stuff, but I am just a good ol' country boy who loves his animals. Anyway, I got off track there. What are your plans for the day? Come on, let's go grab some coffee. I just made some in the kitchen."

I followed Colt into the massive kitchen that was spotlessly clean. The coffee smelled so good. "Come to think of it Colt, I am hungry. Is that breakfast offer still on the table?"

"Sure, I can whip us up something or other. Do you like omelets?" he asked me while reaching for the eggs.

"Not really," I said.

Colt stopped and looked at me, with that deer in the headlights look. "Oh okay, well..."

"I'm just messing with ya Colt! Of course I like omelets; see, I have a sense of humor too!" I said with a smile. "I'll set the table while you cook. Sound good?"

We enjoyed a breakfast of omelets, strawberries and cream, and coffee. When we finished, I had begun to clear the table when Colt asked, "Have you talked to him yet?"

The question caught me so off guard that I asked, "Who?"

"Oliver—your husband."

"No, not yet." It's too soon for me, Colt."

"I understand," he said as he followed me to the sink. "When the time is right," he said. Colt looked at me then, and said, "Do you know how to ride?"

"Ride what?" I asked.

"A horse, of course," he said.

"Well, not really, but I would love to try," I said.

"Okay, let's go then. Come on Alex, I will teach you how to ride. I followed him out to the pink barn and saddled up Ms. Lacy for a ride.

"Ms. Lacy is an old gentle mare and will be good for your first time riding." As we headed out to the

pasture, Colt looked at me and said, "What's your story?"

And with that I proceeded to tell him the whole story, which was now my life. I told him about meeting Oliver at a summer job, me being older and going off to college without him, him graduating early so he could be with me in college; everything I could think of came out of my mouth. For whatever reason, I felt very comfortable with Colt, and even though I had just met him a day ago, it was like he was supposed to be in my life. I just didn't realize how much I would come to love and appreciate his friendship.

Colt rode alongside me, listening to me quietly and without any harsh words about Oliver. A part of me wanted to hear him say something bad, but he did not.

I had no idea how long we had been riding. I had lost all track of time when Colt said, "We'd better head back before the sun goes down. We need to give the horses a rest and find something to eat.

I hadn't even thought of eating. I was so engrossed in telling my story that when I did look at my watch, it was already 6:30. We had spent the whole day out riding and looking at this gorgeous little place on the other side of the lake. Colt's ranch was a thing of beauty, and it was obvious that he, and his family before him, had taken much pride and great care of this land.

We got back to the pink barn, took care of the horses, and I started to walk to my car, thanking Colt for such a great day. I felt relaxed, a little tired, and hungry. He looked at me and said, "Where ya going? I thought we were going to find some dinner. Remember, I owe you a dinner."

We both laughed, and I said, "You fed me breakfast; your debt, kind sir, has been paid in full." I thanked him again and walked to my car.

"Sure I can't change your mind about dinner?" he asked.

"No, I have stolen your entire day and I need a bath. I do kinda smell like horses!" I smiled and got in my car and went back to the cabin.

Chapter 7

I hadn't even checked my cell phone all day. When I did, I saw that Kacee had called like a million times, so I knew it was time to call her back and let her know what was going on. I decided to get a shower first, and then find something quick for supper. After I had settled in, I picked up the phone and called Kacee.

Little Emy answered the phone. "Hey Aunt Alex! How are you?" she asked. "Mommy is eating too much ice cream right now, but she said to bring her the phone." I couldn't help but giggle; Emy was such a precious child and I loved her dearly.

Kacee got the phone from Emy and informed me that she was not eating too much ice cream. We both laughed, both of us knowing she *was* eating too much ice cream.

"So let me guess," I said, "your favorite flavor this week is…whatever you grabbed from the creamery. Am I correct Kacee?"

"You know I love all flavors! There is no favorite in my world." We both laughed again, then silence came over the phone. "Alex," Kacee said softly, "what happened?"

"You know, Kacee, how you look at Emy and realize she is your world and how much that child means to you?"

"Yes of course I do," Kacee said.

"Well, I saw that in Oliver's eyes the afternoon I met his daughter." Silence came over the phone, and I knew at that point Kacee had no idea what to say. "Yes Kacee, you did hear me correctly," I said, as if I were answering a question she had asked. "Oliver has a beautiful little girl. Her name is Meghan and she is a little over 4 years old. She has long blonde hair and big green eyes, and she loves to swing in my back yard on the swing that Oliver hung years ago. Kacee, I am sure she would love to play with Emy sometime."

"Have you lost your mind Alex?" Kacee stammered. "Oliver has a daughter? You have met her? You have looked into her green eyes? She swung on your backyard swing? Playdate with Emy? What? No!" Kacee exclaimed. "You and Oliver are, well, you and Oliver. Now you are you and Oliver and his daughter?"

I couldn't help but giggle as my eyes were filling with tears. "Yes, I have met her; yes, she has green eyes; yes, she has swung on my swing in the yard. But the reality is, I don't know if it is me and Oliver anymore."

"Alex, I can't believe Oliver had an affair. That cheating bastard! That low life! That creep!"

I had to stop Kacee there, as I knew this could go on for quite some time. "Kacee, this was very difficult for Oliver to tell me, and to be honest, I am still processing what all the realities are. I always knew he wanted children, and I guess I looked at it too casually; you know, if it was meant to be then we would be parents. I didn't fully embrace his dream of parenthood; I guess because it had just not happened."

"Alex," Kacee interrupted, "You are being so mature and adult about this, and to be honest, I don't think I can be that mature right now! Alex, that man, your husband, made a child with another woman and then just brings her into your life? That is so, so wrong!" I knew before I told her that I would have to help Kacee calm down and focus. I loved Kacee dearly and she was my best friend, but she was also a challenge at times. Her heart was always in the right place, but sometimes her mouth didn't play follow the leader too well.

"Kacee, Oliver and Meghan's mother had a one-night event when she was in town touring Oliver's hospital."

"Sounds more like she was touring your husband!"

"It certainly sounds that way, but Kacee, it does take two. Oliver feels terrible about the betrayal but is thrilled to be a father. I can't hate him, I just can't! I don't like any of this, but I can't hate him." I continued to tell Kacee all the details that I had until I realized we had been on the phone for 3 hours, and once again I was exhausted!! I told Kacee that I would give her a call in a couple of days and we would talk more then.

"As I started to hang up, Kacee said, "I hate to bring this up, but I am going to anyway. We have a showing in 2 weeks. Do you want me to cancel our reservations and plan to go to the next one?"

"Oh no," I almost yelled in her ear, "We won't cancel anything. This upcoming show is a huge event and we have to be there to complete our upcoming line. Don't cancel anything, and we will talk more in a couple of days. Hey Kacee, I love you girl."

"I love you too Alex," she said, and we both hung up the phone. Everything business seemed to flood into my mind. We had to be at the showing! The little retail chain I had joined so many years ago was now a fashion icon all by itself. We had gone from just buying other's designs to creating our own. I still could not sew, but I knew what lines looked good on what body type. That was the talent I used to get me to the position of Senior Purchasing Executive, and I was also one of the major shareholders in this company. Our plans to introduce our own fashion school was in the works, and the magazine was set to come out next fall. There were so many irons in the fire for me. I thought, *maybe that's why I missed Oliver's signs.*

In my heart, I did realize that I shared the blame for putting our marriage in the place it was now.

"It's wasn't just you," I said to Oliver as if he were standing there. "It was me too. I didn't pay your dreams as much attention as I did my own."

Wow, I thought, *how selfish of me, to totally ignore the man I loved the deepest and desired the most, just to put my goals ahead of ours, his, whoever's!* "Wait," I said out loud, "I didn't cheat! I didn't make a child with another person! Am I crazy to think I share some of the blame?" I decided to put my mind and body to rest for the evening and went to bed.

Chapter 8

I woke up with the sun shining through the bedroom windows and the warmth of the sun on my face. I went to the kitchen to make some coffee, and then headed for the shower. Suddenly, I had a design jump into my head, and I knew that I had to put my idea on paper. I wasn't a designer, I was a buyer, but this was good, if I do say so myself. Then I laughed to myself and thought, *who would buy this? Oh, wait I would!* I laughed and headed for my shower.

After a quick shower and a long time spent enjoying my coffee, I decided that I needed to get some work done and get focused on what this next showing was going to bring to my life, and what I was going to bring to my life. I worked most of the morning and afternoon on comparables, locations, and budgets.

I looked up from the table to realize it was almost 6 pm and I had gotten lost in my work. For me, that was a good feeling. Speaking of feeling, my stomach was growling and I realized I hadn't had anything but coffee all day. It was definitely time to find something to eat. I had bought groceries but was not in the mood to cook, so I loaded up my laptop and decided to enjoy one of the local restaurants.

I was not really sure what I wanted, so I chose Mom and Pop's, a quaint little place that Oliver and I frequented almost every time we came up here. I loved the fact they served a daily special and they were very quick to tell you how good it was. I found a parking place, gathered my purse and laptop, and went into the restaurant. I immediately noticed the new paint job, the new modern atmosphere, and that

Mom and Pop's was no longer the name of this establishment.

I guess I looked a little confused when a young man came over and asked me how many in my party. *How many do you see? Yes, I am here alone, what about it?* "One," I answered, and he led me to a corner table. The waitress brought my menu and asked for my drink order.

I asked, "Why the changes in here? Last time we were here it was Mom and Pop's," I said, without really giving her a chance to answer my question.

"Pop passed away, and Mom couldn't run it without him, so she sold it to a guy from the city. He doesn't come up here too much, but it keeps me in a job, and I am thankful for that!" the waitress said with a smile. "Now what did you say you wanted to drink?" she asked.

"Oh, I guess I didn't tell you, did I?" and we both laughed. "Water...water will be fine."

She stood there looking at me with a quizzical look on her face, "Yes," I asked.

"Well, you're seated at a table for one, and you said last time you were here...is someone joining you? Do I need to get another menu?"

"Oh, no, it will be just me. Thanks." I got my laptop set up and began working again. I was starting to get excited about the upcoming show and knew I wanted to present our very first line of fashion ideas to the world, with hopes of it being great! I am very comfortable with the purchasing of other top designers' ideas, but these were our designs that would be on the runway also. Very exciting and scary time; our fashion house will go from just buying and selling product to providing our own line: the line that will carry our company name. Yes, this is exciting, and

any other time I would be inclined to call Oliver and talk this over with him; to share my thoughts, worries and excitement with him, but that, I guess, is not to be right now. Right now... I wondered how long right now was going to be.

I was lost in work and thought when my dinner arrived. It smelled so good. I became lost in my food at that point. Work would just have to wait, and my stomach was telling me what was more important right then. After enjoying a wonderful meal, I gathered my work and purse, and went to pay the check. The young man who had seated me asked me if everything was good, and I assured him that it was and that I would be seeing them again. With a smile, he handed me back my change and I went to the car to go back to the cabin.

I really did love the scenery here; everything almost looked like time stood still here. The lake, the woods, the gravel roads, all of this seemed so comfortable to me. I enjoyed living in the suburbs, just minutes away from the city and everything in the world you could possibly want or need, but there was just something about the country that called to my spirit. I found peace and calm here, when I didn't realize I was missing it.

As I pulled up in the driveway to the cabin, I realized it had been a long time since I had been back to my hometown. I sat there thinking, *maybe I need to go back to Iowa for a while. Maybe after this next showing. Maybe I will go see my family and spend some time with them and remember where I came from.*

"I will do that," I said to myself as I walked up the stairs and unlocked the door. It was a bit chilly, so I built a fire and snuggled up on the couch for a while.

I awoke the next morning, having slept on the couch all night. I was a bit stiff, but still just feeling like it was time to get my day started.

I showered, dressed, and went for my now daily walk around the lake. I was enjoying the beauty of what this place had to offer when I realized it had been 2 weeks since I had spoken to Oliver. I felt that missing him feeling in my heart and thought I should pick up the phone and call him, at least to tell him where I was and that I was okay. Then I remembered Colt saying he had called Oliver when he found my checkbook outside the local store. He knew where I was, but he hadn't bothered to call and see about me. I wasn't sure that I wanted to hear from him, but still it made me angry to know he hadn't called. I didn't screw up this marriage, this was all him and his cheating ways. Cheating ways...sounded like a country song title and I couldn't help but laugh out loud.

I knew the time had come for me to go back to our home and discuss my future with Oliver. On my way back to the cabin to pack up my stuff Colt came up the hill on his horse.

"Heading back home are ya, Alex?"

I looked up at him on that beautiful horse and laughed, "How did you know?"

"Were you going to come by and say goodbye before you left?" he asked.

"Actually, I was going to invite you to breakfast with me, Colt. How about I cook...no wait how about I buy you breakfast in town?"

He smiled and said he couldn't tie his horse up in town anymore because some of the folks complained. We both laughed and I told him I would swing by his place and pick him up.

Chapter 8

"You got a date, Alex. See you in a bit." Colt tipped his hat, turned around and rode off toward the pink barn.

Chapter 9

I went back to the cabin, touched up my makeup, and was heading out when I saw Oliver standing in the driveway. He began to walk up the steps without saying a word, just looking at me with what looked like a storm in his eyes.

"Oliver? What are you doing here?" He didn't say anything, just stepped right up to me on the deck, put his arms around me and began to cry. My first instinct was to comfort him and hold him. It came so naturally that I had to make myself pull away from him. "Oliver, I am on my way to pick up a friend for breakfast. Why are you here? Why are you crying? Is everything okay? Is your daughter okay?"

He looked at me and said that everything was not okay and that he had missed me and was so sorry for hurting me. I had to stop him right there, "Oliver, I need to talk to you. There is no denying that, but right now I have plans. I will be back later, and if you're still here then we can talk."

With that I went down the stairs, got in my car and drove off. My heart was racing, and my thoughts were going even faster. I wasn't sure that I had done the right thing by leaving him standing there, but I wasn't sure staying was the right thing either.

I headed to Colt's place and practically missed the turn I was going so fast. When I got to the house, Colt was ready to go, with a big smile on his face. He looked at me, and before I had a chance to say anything he said, "Oliver is here isn't he?"

I sat there staring at him. "How did you know? I seem to ask you that a lot," I said.

Colt looked at me. "Alex," he said, "what happened?"

"Well, nothing really. He walked up the stairs, put his arms around me and began to cry. I pulled away from him, told him I had a breakfast date and if he was still there when I got back we could talk. Then I came to your place. I may have knocked your mail box down when I turned in your drive. Sorry."

Colt looked at me with concern and laughter in his eyes. You may have knocked it down? You don't know?" He let out a chuckle, "Alex, let's go. I am hungry and you need to talk, but how about I drive?" We both laughed and Colt slid behind the wheel of my car.

I don't let anyone drive my car, but for whatever reason I was so comfortable with this man that it felt like I had known him all my life.

"Colt, I looked at Oliver as he was walking up the stairs, and it was almost like looking at a stranger. I had no idea what to say to my husband, who stood before me crying and looking so sad. All I could think of was to leave; just get in the car and leave this bad situation behind me. I guess that is what I thought I would do when I came up here a few weeks ago. I ran, Colt. I didn't solve anything, I just ran away."

"You know, Alex, when Cassie passed away that's all I wanted to do – run away. In many respects, it would have done me good, but I didn't run. Instead, I stayed and hid out on the farm. I figured that if she was going to be gone, I would have to stay there and keep everything running just like she would have. I don't know if it's right or wrong to run away or to stay put, but when your heart is broken, you just have to figure out a way to survive. Life has its struggles, but we survive and continue on."

56

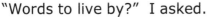

"Words to live by?" I asked.

Colt looked at me and smiled, "Yes they are," he answered.

We drove into town and got some breakfast and talked for hours. I had truly forgotten about Oliver until I saw him walk through the café door.

He slowly walked up to the table where Colt and I were with an unsure look on his face. He said, "Alex? I thought you were coming back to our cabin."

"Oliver, I'm sorry. I lost track of time. I did have every intention of coming back to the cabin to talk." Oliver looked at Colt the entire time I was speaking to him. "Oliver, this is Colt, my new friend. Colt, this is Oliver, my husband."

Colt stood and extended his hand to Oliver. "Nice to meet you, Oliver." As they shook hands, Colt reached for a chair for Oliver and told him to join us.

Oliver stopped him. No, I don't mean to interrupt your...your breakfast. I just wanted to make sure Alex was alright."

"I am fine as you can see. Funny you should ask now, but yes Oliver, I am fine."

"Alex, I need to talk to you. We need to go home, or at least to our cabin, and work this out."

Colt grabbed the check and said, "I will be right back." I tried to take it from him, but he walked away rather quickly.

"Alex," Oliver said, "I have missed you so much. I don't know how to...even begin to make this right."

"How's your daughter?" I asked. The words spewed out of my mouth. "How is Ellen?"

Colt came back to the table. "Alex, Oliver, I'm just going to catch a ride back to the farm. I'll see y'all later on. It was nice meeting you, Oliver. I hope to see you around for a while."

The look on my face was that of shock and anger for Colt. I had told him my life story; how Oliver had betrayed our vows, created a child with another woman, and he says hope to see you around?

Colt looked at me and said, "Life has its struggles, but we survive and continue on." And with that, he turned and walked out the café door.

Oliver and I both stared at the exit that Colt had made use of, and decided it was time for us to leave as well. We walked to the door and Oliver went to get the door of his car for me.

"I have my car, Oliver. I will meet you at the cabin." As I drove back up to the cabin, my thoughts were fuzzy and racing. I was not sure what this was going to turn into with Oliver.

Oliver got there first and opened my door for me as he always did. We walked up the stairs together, with him opening the door for me as he always did, and him taking my coat as he always did. I guess it was just our way, but right now it seemed so awkward and forced. Nothing seemed to just flow like it always had. We were trying to be normal, and that was a whole new feeling for me. But in the last several weeks, I'd had many new feelings come over me, thanks to Oliver.

As we sat down on the sofa, Oliver turned to me and said, "Alexandra, I wanted to call you. I wanted to come here immediately after your friend Colt called. I wanted to hold you in my arms and beg for your forgiveness, but I didn't. I didn't because I found myself in a place that I am not familiar with. In all the years we have been together Alex, I have always known my life wasn't complete unless you were in it. I know I have put us in this situation, but I know in my

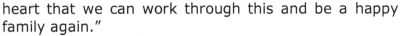

heart that we can work through this and be a happy family again."

"You mean the two of us, or the three of us, or even the four of us?"

Oliver stared at me and stuttered, "I don't...four?

No, no, you, me and Meghan."

"What about Ellen?" I asked. "What, every other weekend Meghan comes to our house, a couple of weeks in the summer she spends with her daddy?"

"I am confused. What does Ellen have to do with us, Alex?"

"She has everything to do with us, Oliver. She is the mother of your child." The words stung him like bee stings and tasted like vinegar coming out of my mouth. "What about Ellen, Oliver?"

"Sweetheart," Oliver said to me, "there is no Ellen in our family. Ellen and I will be friends and raise a daughter together, but separately. I am not in love with Ellen and she is not in love with me. We made a mistake that created someone I would not change, but would I have rather had Meghan with you? Of course I would have! If I could back up Alex..."

"But you can't Oliver," I interrupted, "You can't."

"It won't be difficult, Alex. Meghan doesn't live that close to us, so she won't be there all the time. I know you will love her too, once you get to know her. You will be a great step mom!"

"Oliver, you need to understand this. I have no doubt I would love your daughter, but she would also not be my daughter. I would always be the step mom and that's just not something I signed on for. Meghan is a beautiful little girl, and you need to spend as much time with her as possible. Maybe you should sell the house and move closer to her. Your job will take you anywhere, and you can watch her grow up. I realize you say that you and Ellen are just friends, and I am happy for the both of you, but I don't know that I could be that mature in this situation. I don't see where I fit into your family now."

"Alexandra, what are you saying? You don't want to try? You don't love me? You can't love our daughter?"

"Oliver," I shouted, "She is not our daughter, she is yours...yours and someone else's! Not Mine! Second of all, yes I love you, why do you think it is so difficult to say goodbye to you?"

"Goodbye? Alexandra? Are you saying goodbye to me, to our life together?"

We both sat there looking at each other with disbelief in our eyes. Had I really just said that? Did those words really just come out of my mouth?

"Oliver, when I said my vows to you, I meant every word I said. I meant you and I forever, I meant until death do us part. Did you?"

"Of course I did." His voice was almost a whisper as he stared at me. "I mean them now. Alex, I can't imagine my life without you as my wife."

We were both speechless at that point, neither one of us sure what to say. Oliver rose to his feet and silently walked towards the door. I remained seated and quiet on the couch. Oliver turned and looked at me. "Alexandra, I know I have hurt you, and I will never be able to say I'm sorry enough to make it up to you. I love you with all of my heart, and I know you still love me too. You don't just throw away all these years like it never even happened. Our marriage is important to me, and I hope you will want to work on the future together. I don't expect you to forgive and

forget right away, but maybe over time you will see that this really can work for us."

"All three of us?" I asked.

"Yes, Alex, all three of us. I have no intention of selling our home. That is where you and I and Meghan belong. I know this may not be the best time to tell you this, but Ellen is letting Meghan come live with me. We have discussed this to great lengths, and Meghan and I are both very excited about being under the same roof full time. I do love my little girl, Alex..."

I stopped him there. "I know you do Oliver, and I know she loves you dearly. This will be good, for you and her to spend more time together.

"I think it will too, Alex. We just need you to come home and be with us."

"Oliver," I rose and walked to him, "Please don't push me. I have so much to sort out with all of this and work. I have a very important showing coming up soon and the deadlines are getting closer."

"Alex, does Colt have anything to do with this?" Oliver asked.

The anger in my eyes must have flashed like lightning bolts, because Oliver took a step back from me. "For you to ask if there is someone else is more than ironic, Oliver." I steamed with anger at the very thought of him questioning my loyalty. "I didn't cheat on you, and I certainly didn't have a child with another man, and yet you have the nerve to stand there and ask me something like that? Oliver! No, Colt has nothing to do with any decision I have or will make. He is a nice man who lost the love of his life when his wife passed away. He is not just someone I am looking to have a relationship with. I will tell you this much, Oliver. I am very comfortable around Colt, and you should be so lucky to have a friend like him as well. I need to get back to work; I have to be in New York next week and I need to focus on this trip."

Oliver leaned forward and gave me a kiss on the cheek, and whispered, "I love you Alex." With that, he walked out the door. My heart was breaking and a part of me wanted to run after him, tell him to stay, and that it would be okay, but I could not make my feet move. It was like I was in cement and had no control over my legs; they just would not move.

Chapter 10

I stood there as the tears began to flow down my face. How did all this happen? Why was I being put through this? I had never experienced this kind of pain and uncertainly in my life, and I really wanted to wake up from this nightmare that had now become the unraveling of my life.

My perfect life I just kept saying to myself, *my perfect life shot to hell, because of someone else's actions.* I wiped my eyes and reached for my car keys. I knew where I wanted to be right now, and that was with Colt. I needed to hear some of his comforting sayings and let this wave of pain pass.

I knocked on Colt's front door and waited for him to answer. I stood there shaking from the chill in the evening air and weak from all the crying. When Colt opened the door, the normally smiling face had a look of uncertainty and caution. He motioned me in and we walked to the warmth of the fireplace where I stood in shock, because Oliver was there.

"Wait, what are you doing here? You just met Colt this morning. Why are you in his house? I am confused. Wait...I will just go. I am not sure what's going on, but I need to go." I ran towards the door.

Colt put his hand on the door and looked me in the eyes. "Alex, Oliver came over after you and he talked, and I was being a friend to him just like I am to you. I think you two need some more time to talk about things, and it just so happens that I have a large pot of stew that is ready for eating."

"Colt, I should have not just dropped in on you. I am so sorry, but I need to go. I am just not ready for this and I'm not ready to share your friendship with Oliver."

Oliver was standing there in the hall and after hearing my words, he too apologized to Colt for coming over and said it was time for him to go back home. Colt assured both of us that we were welcome there and the best way to work things out was to talk them out. I looked at Oliver and opened the door for him to leave. Oliver extended his hand to Colt and thanked him for his hospitality, then got in his car and drove off.

I turned to Colt with anger and confusion on my face, and as I began to speak, the words just turned to tears and sobbing. Colt put his arm around me and we walked to the kitchen. "There's nothing like stew to make you feel like everything will be okay," he said. I really wasn't very hungry but at his insistence I began to eat. "Funny thing," Colt said, "Stew is just this and that of things that work together. Kinda like people. You never know who and what fits together."

"Colt, why was Oliver here?"

"You know, Alex, my wife always said I had that face, the face that strangers took to, the face that said I will be there for you. I guess she was right. Oliver called me on the way from your place and asked if we could talk. I of course told him to come on over. He wanted to see if I was the one that would try to take his place. He realized soon after being here that I would never be in love with anyone the way I was with my Cassandra. Then he began to open up about what all was on his mind - you and his little girl. Alex, Oliver loves you dearly and knows he made things in your world go all pear-shaped. I am not telling you this for you to go back to him. I'm just sayin' that he blames himself for everything and takes full responsibility for

Chapter 10

all the deceit and craziness that y'all are going through." Colt leaned in and said, "Can you honestly tell me it was his fault entirely?"

The question caught me so off guard that I could not even think of a response. I stood up without speaking and walked to the door, reached for the knob, looked back at Colt, and walked out to my car. *Why isn't it his fault?* I thought to myself. *Why should I have to see his side of this? Why, Why, Why?* I asked myself. I drove back to the cabin in yet another personal haze. I thought my husband of so many years was the one I could always turn to, and that proved to be not true. Then I met Colt. I didn't ask for him to come into my life, and I thought I could turn to him, and yet after that question I am wondering, is it me? Am I just that poor a judge of character that I can't find a decent man in this world who will just be there for me? Who won't cheat on me, or who will listen as a friend and take my side?

There was one man I knew I could always depend on to love me, so I picked up the phone. "Hello Dad. How are you?" I had always had the greatest parents and I knew I was very blessed to have them. I had friends growing up whose parents had divorced, or even worse, didn't divorce when they really should have, and I was fortunate to come home to two parents that loved and provided very well for me. I have three older brothers whom I love very much but all three are pretty much are in agreement that I was the most spoiled. I would always disagree with them on that subject but we all knew it was the truth. Dad and I talked for a good while about work, life, good things. I wasn't going to burden him with my problems, I just needed to hear his voice. With that, I realized I was not alone in this world. I told Dad good night and that I loved him and would see him soon, and hung up the phone.

I began to clean up and pack up. It was time for me to go to New York for the show and get back on track. I called Kacee to confirm our reservations and told her I would see her in NYC. Normally Kacee would arrive to whatever destination we were going a day or two ahead of me to make sure everything was in place, but this time I decided it was my turn to handle the details. I packed my bags and went to bed. This had been an exhausting day, and I was ready now to put it behind me.

Chapter 11

I was up before the sun came up and headed out on the interstate for the drive. Normally I parked my car at the airport, but since my world was now a little out of focus I decided the drive would do me good. Plus, I wouldn't have to get a cab in New York, which was impossible most of the time. The drive up would take about 10 hours, and I loved the thought of seeing the countryside that I had missed so much of by flying over it.

I thought to myself, *if you really want to see the countryside on this drive, get off the interstate and take the back roads*. I had the time and the GPS, so that was my plan now. I programmed the GPS where I needed to end up and headed onward. I drove past many places that looked like they belonged on a Hallmark card. The beauty of this great country was unmatchable in my opinion; I had traveled all over the world but loved the look and feel of the United States more than anywhere. It was time for me to take in all the states, and see all that this country had to offer, but that would have to wait. I had just hit New York State and the traffic was less than majestic, but this is what makes us who we are. We are a country on the go constantly, and all those places we are going are waiting for us to get there.

I arrived at the hotel and checked into my room. Kacee had done well, as usual. This room was amazing, and I looked forward to getting to the venue to choose our area to present our line and to see where our viewing seats were. I had been to New York many times, and most of these shows were held in the same venues, but this was a new one for me. I was excited to see what it had to offer. We had always selected seats to view the new fashions, but it took many years to get into the advantage seats. Those were the ones reserved for the big fashion buyers, those that had a much larger budget than we did. Our time was now, and we had earned our place among the established fashion elite. I was so excited about presenting our new line, and I needed to see how this part of the expo went.

I found our models' dressing area, and our new fashions would be delivered later in the afternoon. Security would be on hand as each designer's product was delivered because people had been known to accidently steal from other designers right off the rack. I had heard that happened on a regular basis and the given excuse was it was an accident. No other excuses were ever given; this seemed to be the norm. It was a form of flattery, of course, to know that someone liked your design so much they would accidently steal it, but on many occasions it was not flattery, it was just leaving a designer with a smaller showing than the others, and that never looked good for that designer.

I was still in the dressing room when Kacee walked in. "What do you think of this place?" she asked. I was startled and jumped when I heard Kacee's voice.

"I didn't even hear you come in," I said to her as both of us were laughing at my reaction to hearing her.

"It's a great place," Kacee said, and our dressing room is the second door from the stage. That took some finagling, but I got it done," she boasted.

"You did a wonderful job Kacee. Everything looks amazing. I love the fact that after all these years

of earning our advantage seats, we are also presenting our first line. There is so much that we have to be thankful for. We have come a long way, my friend." I looked at Kacee and smiled, knowing so much of our success was due to her.

Kacee was probably the most organized person I knew. She was very detail oriented and was excellent under pressure. Her only flaw was her addiction to ice cream. Breakfast, lunch or dinner, Kacee would be eating ice cream. It usually didn't even matter what kind, and she never had to worry about her figure as she had an amazing shape that stayed the same with little or no effort. I on the other hand had to work out on a regular basis to keep me in check. I guess if that was Kacee's worst attribute then that was a pretty complete life.

Kacee and her husband Kyle had been married for about 2 years when we met, and the love they shared was beautiful. They had such respect and concern for one another that I found myself hoping Oliver and I were that strong as a couple as well. When they found out they were pregnant with Emy they were so excited and couldn't wait to tell Oliver and me. I was so happy for them and so was Oliver, but there was a sense of sadness in him. I didn't really understand until now. Having to hide the fact that he had a child already with another woman would not have been the best news to share at that time. Kacee said they wanted more children but that time would be a long way away for them as Emy kept them on their toes most of the time. Yes, I was very fortunate to have Kacee on my team. She was also my very best friend with whom I had shared my life for so many years.

♥♥♥♥♥♥♥♥♥♥♥♥♥

I stood there staring at Kacee with a glassy look on my face. When she turned around, she said, "What are you looking at me like that for?" I just snickered and told her I was glad she was here. "Well, we have a lot to do tonight if we are going to be ready for tomorrow's show." Kacee brought out her tablet and we began strategizing every minute of tonight and tomorrow.

Tonight the clothes would arrive and we would need to sort by model and time to make full use of the natural light that would come in during the show. The lighting was so important because many of the designs were of color contrasting material. These shows could go on for quite some time and you always wanted your designs to be the very first and the very last. Kacee had arranged for our line to come out first, which was almost impossible for a first time showing. Our show stopper would, however, not be at the very end of the production. Since we were new in the design field, we had to wait our turn one more time. I was very pleased with the lineup, and Kacee would be there to direct the models as I was seated for the buying process. This was going to be very exciting and extremely busy.

After many hours at the venue we decided it was time for some dinner and a break. We got in my car and started to pull out when Kacee laughed and looked at me. "Have you ever driven in New York? Why did you bring your car? The parking here is impossible, and you know you can't parallel park worth a darn! What were you thinking?" Kacee laughed and buckled herself in, and then, turning to me said, "You're not going home after this show is over, are you? Where are you going Alex?"

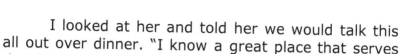

I looked at her and told her we would talk this all out over dinner. "I know a great place that serves the best chicken pasta bake, except for mine of course."

We both laughed and drove to the restaurant. It was quiet and not too crowded. I was relieved to see that, as I knew Kacee would be waiting impatiently with many questions, some of which I was pretty sure I did not yet have the answers to. We were seated quickly and I began to scan the menu when in typical Kacee fashion, the barrage of questions began. I couldn't help but laugh out loud at Kacee as I started to fill her in on my world and where I was right now. I told her all about Colt and his asking me if I truly believe everything was Oliver's fault. I told her all about Oliver's surprise visit and our talk. I told her everything I could think of and what I had decided and not decided to do yet. Kacee and I sat there for hours as they flew by, and I soon realized that her being there was what I needed at that point in my life. I thanked her for listening to me, being my friend, for all her hard work in the fashion house alongside of me, and mostly for just being who she is. I put my hand on hers, looked her in the eye and told her how much I loved her. Kacee held my hand and told me the feeling was more than mutual, and she was so fortunate to have me as her best friend.

Kacee looked at her watch and almost jumped out of her skin. "It's 10:00! We have to go to the venue! We have to go sign for the designs and get them in order." This is the part that she always handled, and I thought I had everything taken care of. We scurried to the car, drove like crazy women, and got back to the venue. Other designers were already there and the excitement was in the air. Our product was just being brought in as we arrived and Kacee signed for them. We headed to our dressing room to inventory and put the dresses in order for the models. Everything had arrived and was in excellent condition. We put every dress, every accessory, every pair of shoes, every everything in order, and we were now ready for tomorrow's show. Kacee and I were exhausted and ready to go back to our hotel at this point.

As we drove back to the hotel, Kacee looked at me with that look that said she needed ice cream. "Oh my gosh, Kacee! Are you serious? Its 2 in the morning and it's time for us to go..."

"To the ice cream parlour!" Kacee finished my sentence and I knew it was hopeless; we were now on a mission to find an ice cream parlor at 2 in the morning in New York City. I was shocked when we happened upon one; Kacee looked at me like a child would when they had just proven their parent wrong.

"Okay, Kacee...let's go get ice cream." We sat there eating and finishing up the last of our to do list for in the morning. I thought, *who am I kidding? It's already morning and we haven't even gone to bed yet.* We arrived back at the hotel around 3:30 and I asked for a wakeup call at 6 am.

I got to my room, took my shoes off, and collapsed into my bed. I couldn't remember being this tired for a long time, and I couldn't wait to shut my eyes. I crawled into bed and felt every muscle in my body relax as I drifted off to sleep.

When the wakeup call came, it felt like I had just gotten into bed, but I knew it was going to be such a memorable day that I had to get a move on. I showered, brushed my teeth, and was finishing getting dressed when Kacee knocked on the door. I truly don't

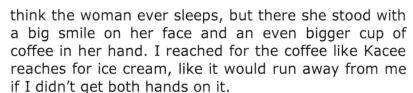

think the woman ever sleeps, but there she stood with a big smile on her face and an even bigger cup of coffee in her hand. I reached for the coffee like Kacee reaches for ice cream, like it would run away from me if I didn't get both hands on it.

We made our way out of the hotel and into New York City traffic. Normally I would not have relished the thought of all this, but for some reason it was so exciting for me. We made it to the venue without any concerns and that was an accomplishment in itself, I thought. We were one of the first ones there and it was even more exciting for me as I decided to sneak a peek at some of the other designers' master pieces.

I was walking towards the next dressing room down from ours when Kacee grabbed me. "What are you doing?" she asked. "Have you lost your mind? We are not allowed in there and we are not the kind of people that sneak peeks at other people's fashions! Jeez, Alex, what has gotten into you?"

I felt like I was in seventh grade again getting caught passing notes in Biology class. "Alright, but just know if someone's designs look better than ours, it's your fault," I said with a smirk on my face.

"Okay, so noted," Kacee said, "Now let's get busy." As the models arrived, we dressed them and gave them their instructions. Knowing Kacee was here to handle this part, I went to mingle with the other buyers and prepare for the show to begin. Several of the other buyers had heard that we were producing our first line and many of them wished us luck.

As the show started and the models came out wearing our designs, I felt such pride and completeness that we had made this line. Our fashions were fabulous and the buyers were on their Blackberries placing orders before the show even really got started. Every order that was being placed for our line was directly connected to my Blackberry, as well as the intake line back at the fashion house. There were so many notifications coming across my phone that I had to turn it off and concentrate on the next designer's line that was coming down the runway. After all, I was there to purchase as well as present. So many of the new fashions were so beautiful and the presentations were flawless. This was definitely the best show I had been to in quite a while.

Chapter 12

About 2 hours into the showing, we went to intermission and I was paged to the front desk. I assumed that Kacee was going to fill me in on the goings on in the dressing room and we would then continue to watch the remaining show together. I arrived at the desk, but instead of seeing Kacee, I saw Colt standing there with a beautiful bouquet of roses. "Colt," I almost whispered his name, "what are you doing in New York?"

"Well, it's nice to see you too, Alex" he laughed. "You can take the flowers anytime now. They are getting heavy!" We both laughed.

"I'm sorry! Thank you; they are gorgeous. Yellow is my favorite color and roses are my favorite flower! How did you know that? Oh, you have been talking to Oliver haven't you?" I asked. "The two of you getting closer, are you? How nice for the both of you! I can't believe you would come here on his behalf, Colt. I am just..."

"You are just what?" Colt asked. "Alex, I have said it before, but sometimes you are hard to be nice to. Yes, I have talked with Oliver. No, he didn't ask me to bring these to you, but he did ask if I had heard from you. I told him no, since you have not bothered to return my calls. Alex, I have to wonder what kind of people you consider friends. Just because we have an argument, we are no longer friends? What is that? Wasn't high school a long time ago?"

Colt leaned in, kissed my cheek and said, "I will see you later."

I stood there staring at him. "Colt...wait! Please don't go. I am so sorry. I am very happy you are here.

Thank you again for the flowers, and I am sorry I haven't returned your calls. I didn't know what to say to you because I was angry at what you asked me about Oliver and I... and I just wanted to get away. You actually made me do some thinking and you're right, it's not all his fault, kinda."

We both smiled and at that point the lights lowered. That was my cue to get back to my seat for the rest of the show. I looked at Colt and asked him to join me for the remaining portion of the showing. He smiled and shook his head no. "Now if y'all were modeling jeans and boots I might stay around, but I think I will head back to my hotel."

"Wait...are you staying in New York tonight? Where are you staying? Do you have plans for dinner?" I asked him, hoping the answer was yes.

"I do have plans for dinner; I have a date," Colt said.

"You do?" I asked.

"Don't looked so shocked Alex, jeez!"

I couldn't help but feel let down. "No I am not shocked I was just..."

"Alex," Colt said, "I will pick you up at seven, and with a wink and a smile he turned around and headed out the front entrance.

I couldn't help but giggle like a schoolgirl and realized I had to get to my seat before I missed any more of the show. I slid in beside Kacee and she looked at me with that, where have you been, look. Before she could actually ask me where I had been I whispered, "I will tell you later."

The show lasted another 2 hours, and all the designs more than exceeded my expectations. At the end of every show the designers get to walk down the cat walk and this year I was asked to walk for our

❤ ❤ ❤ ❤ ❤ ❤ ❤ ❤ ❤ ❤ ❤ ❤ ❤

fashion house. We had so many talented designers and we all worked together as a team. Since went under our fashion house label I was the lucky one that got to walk. I was honored and scared to death at the same time. All the models walked so effortlessly and gracefully down the catwalk in their 8-inch heels, never missing their marks or falling on their butts, but this was me going down the runway that could be an entirely different story. When my name was called I strolled out there like I had done it a million times, smiling and waving. I had often made fun of the designers as they always seemed to cry as they made their way down the runway and now as I began my walk, I understood. The tears of pride flowed down my cheeks and I was so overwhelmed by the emotion that I realized why they all cried.

I made my walk, went back to the dressing room, and thanked each and every model and designer for their hard work, professionalism, and dedication to our line. I also sent them all out to dinner at the fashion house's expense. It was such a great feeling, and I knew that despite everything that had taken place in the last few months I was in a good place. I knew there were loose ends to tie up, but I would be okay.

I went to find Kacee and head back to the hotel room to change for dinner with Colt. Kacee looked at me and before I could say anything, she asked, "Why were you late coming back from intermission? You actually missed four brand new styles that came down the catwalk. That could cost us thousands of dollars!"

"I know Kacee, but I am sure you put the order in for me, didn't you?" I asked.

She nodded her head and it was like she could see into my soul. "What?" She asked.

What, what?" I asked her back.

"What is it?" Kacee asked again. "You're keeping something from me...what is it?"

"Okay, okay," I said. "Did you hear me get paged to the front desk earlier?"

"Yeah, I wondered what that was about. Where did you get the yellow roses? Oh and..."

"Kacee," I said, "Shut up for a second and let me tell you." We both laughed and I said, "Anyway, I went to the desk to see why I had been paged and Colt was there with a dozen yellow roses. I was shocked and happy to see him; I had missed him a lot. Funny how much I missed someone whom I have not known that long.

"Anyway," Kacee said, "Keep talking.

I looked at Kacee and realized I had no idea why Colt was here in New York. He didn't tell me the reason. "I am not sure why he is here, but he knew where to find me, and told me that friends don't give up on each other even if they do have an argument."

Kacee laughed loudly and said, "If we gave up on each other each time we had an argument we would have called it quits years ago."

Both of us laughed as we headed for the hotel. It had been a great day and I had so much to be thankful for. I knew God had blessed me, and even though I may not know the path I was going to take, I knew he had me covered. When we reached the hotel it was almost seven, and I knew Colt would be there soon. I told Kacee to hurry and dress for dinner, as she would be joining us and would finally get to meet Colt.

Kacee turned to me and asked, "Are you crazy?"

I answered her back with, "Is that rhetorical?"

Chapter 12

♥ ♥ ♥ ♥ ♥ ♥ ♥ ♥ ♥ ♥ ♥ ♥ ♥ ♥

"Yes!" She yelled and laughed. "I'm going to take a hot bath, order room service, and stay in. Alex, you need to go get dressed for dinner, and you'd better hurry, since I think Colt is already here."

"What?" I asked.

"There is a man staring at you and walking this way."

I turned around and there was Colt walking up to us. "You're early!" I said.

"My Cassandra always said if you're not 15 minutes early, then you're late." Colt replied.

We both smiled at each other and I turned to Kacee to introduce them. "Kacee, this is Colt. Colt, this is Kacee."

Colt leaned in and gave Kacee a small kiss on the cheek. "It's nice to meet you Kacee. I have heard a lot about you."

"I have you as well, Colt." Kacee looked at me with that tell-me-all-about-it-later look and excused herself to go fall into a hot bath.

As I began to walk to the elevator, I turned to speak to Colt and realized he had seated himself in the lobby next to the fireplace. I walked back to him with a quizzical look on my face. "Aren't you coming up with me?" I asked. "I have a beautiful suite, and you would be more comfortable there, wouldn't you?"

Colt looked at me and smiled. "Alex, you are still a married woman, and it would just not look right for me to join you in your fancy room. I'll wait here for you, but you'd better hurry up because I am starving!"

I nodded my head in agreement and hurried to the elevator. I really was blessed to have found a friend in Colt. He was good through and through. I didn't think of him as anything but a friend, and I knew that's the way he thought of me too. I smiled as

I let myself into my room, thinking that even though Oliver's secret had been such an upheaval in my world, I was okay.

I dressed quickly and headed back down to the lobby. Colt was still sitting there waiting for me and let out a whistle that made me laugh out loud. "Stop!" I said, as I waved for him to continue. We both laughed and headed out into the night.

Colt hailed a taxi, and after we climbed in, I turned to him and said, "I have my car you know."

"Yeah, I know; that's why I got the cab," he said with a devilish grin on his face.

"Whatever," I said and grinned back at him.

We pulled up to the restaurant, and the line was out the door and around the block. "Oh my," I said. "It looks like we are in for a wait."

"Did you by chance make reservations?" Colt asked me.

"Now how was I supposed to make reservations, when I had no idea..." I looked at Colt who had that evil grin on his face yet again. I laughed and swung my clutch bag at him, and we slid out of the cab and walked to the door. I assumed we would have to put our names on the list, but the maître d' escorted us right in. I looked at Colt with that look of confusion; he just winked at me and motioned for me to follow the maître d' to our table where we were seated next to the most beautiful fireplace I had ever seen.

When we had settled ourselves in, I looked at Colt and said, "Okay, start talking mister. How do you just so happen to be in New York City the same week I am? How did we just walk past a line that was forever long to get amazing seats in this gorgeous restaurant? There is no way you would have had a reservation

time for us, as we had no idea what time the day's events would wind up. Spill it my friend! Tell me what you are up to!" I tried to give him my mean look, but with the way Colt's eyes were laughing at me I couldn't help but laugh out loud.

"Okay," he said, "I was actually coming to the city anyway. I had business to attend to and decided that I would be here the same time you were so we could talk. I contacted Kacee and asked for your itinerary, and although she was hesitant to give it to me, after I did some sweet talking she let me know your schedule."

"Oh, Kacee," I said. "I swear if she wasn't my best friend..." I looked at Colt and said, "I am so glad she is.

"What kind of business do you have way up here in New York City?" I asked. "You don't like leaving the ranch just to run to town, so I can't imagine what it must have taken to get you to the city."

Colt took a drink of his sweet tea and smirked at me. "Yes Alex, you are correct. I don't like leaving the farm too often, but I happen to have some interests in the city that I personally have to take care of about 4 times a year."

"Okay, what are they?" I asked.

"Well, since you are so nosy, I will tell you. I happen to have a seat on the board of the American Cattleman's Association and there was a meeting that needed my input and my vote, so that was one reason for being here. There is also this little restaurant that I love to come to when I am in the city and we are here tonight."

"So this is one of your favorite places to eat in the city?" I asked him.

"Yes it is. The food is great, the service is wonderful and the atmosphere is very comfortable for me. Cassandra used to love this place, and she insisted we dine here every time we came to New York."

"I understand why she loved it here," I whispered. "Your wife had very good taste, Colt."

"Yes she did. I am not really sure what happened with her taste in men though."

"Yeah, I would have to question that as well," I said with a smirk on my face.

Colt threw his napkin at me just as the waiter was bringing our dinner. Colt looked at his food and then at the waiter and said, "Thank you, Samuel, it looks great!"

"You are so welcome, Mr. Colt. Is there anything else I can get for you right now?"

Colt looked at me and raised his eyebrow. "Anything you need right now, Alex?"

"No, thank you. I am good. It looks amazing and I am so hungry!"

"Then let's eat," Colt said.

After a few moments of pure delight in our dinner I looked at Colt and asked, "The waiter knows you by your first name? You really must come here a lot, or you must have really made an impression on him, since you only come here about 4 times a year."

Colt looked at me and said with a smile, "Cassandra made the impression. I was just along for the ride."

"I can see that," I said with a grin. "I wish I would have had the opportunity to meet Cassandra. The more we talk about her, the more I feel like I know her."

Chapter 12

"Everyone that met her loved her immediately, Alex. She had the most infectious laugh in the world and her taste was impeccable. Speaking of Oliver, have you heard from him?" Colt asked.

"Speaking of Oliver? Who was speaking of Oliver?" I asked, as I almost showered Colt with my water.

Colt couldn't help but laugh at my reaction to his question and asked if I needed some more water. "No, I'm fine." I laughed too. "And no, I have not talked to Oliver in some time now. Have you Colt? Have you spoken with Oliver lately?" I asked.

"Well, now that you bring it up, yes I have."

"Bring it up? I didn't bring him up. "Oh Colt, you are such rascal sometimes."

We both chuckled and Colt looked at me with a sense of seriousness in his face. "Alex, at some point you will need to decide what you are going to do. I can look at you at times and know you're lost without him, and still very angry at the same time. I felt the same way about Cassandra," he said.

"Colt," I said, "Our circumstances are very different, I assure you. Cassandra didn't cheat on you and produce a child with someone else," I said to him.

"No, no, Alex, she didn't, but she did leave me, and I was alone and had to find my way without her. You have the opportunity to not go this alone unless that is what you want to do. The decision is yours to make gal. It just won't be an easy one."

I nodded my head in agreement with his statement as our waiter came back to our table. "Mr. Colt, are you and your friend ready for some dessert?"

"Oh Samuel, you know me too well. What's on the dessert list for this evening?"

"We have an outstanding variety of pure decadency, Mr. Colt, but not to worry we have your favorite, warm apple pie and butter pecan ice cream."

"Samuel, that sounds too good to pass up. Alex, what would you like?" Colt asked.

"Oh, I think I will pass on dessert. Maybe next time," I said with a soft smile.

Colt looked at me with that suit yourself look, and Samuel scooted off towards the kitchen to retrieve Colt's dessert. Samuel was back so quickly I almost felt that the kitchen had this ready even before Colt had ordered. I couldn't help but smile as Colt's face lit up like a child who had just received their biggest Christmas present.

Colt was about 2 bites in when he looked up at me with a kind of startled look on his face. "What?" He asked.

"You're not going to offer me any?" I asked.

"Uh...no! I will get you your own, but I don't share dessert, especially this dessert." We both busted out laughing so loudly that people began to stare at us. We both shushed each other and Colt continued to devour his apple pie and butter pecan ice cream like he didn't have a care in the world.

At that point I guess neither of us did have a care in the world. My first showing of my fashion house's line went exceptionally well, the designs that I purchased were excellent, and I was having a wonderful evening with my friend who, even though I had not known him very long, had become someone very important to me.

"What a wonderful evening this is," I said. "Thank you, Colt, for being here and being such a good friend to me."

"The pleasure is all mine ma'am. I have certainly enjoyed this as well. You ready to go?" Colt asked.

I shook my head yes and we had begun to leave when I looked at Colt and asked, "Are we just going to leave without paying?"

"No worries," he said, "they will just put it on my tab."

"Your tab? Who has a tab anywhere these days?" I asked with shock in my voice. Colt laughed, reached for my hand and escorted me to the door.

"Good night, Mr. Colt," Samuel said.

"Good night, Samuel. See you next time." Colt hailed a cab and we were quickly snarled in traffic, but neither of us seemed to mind as we both looked out our windows at the lights like a couple of folks fresh off the farm. I looked at Colt and laughed out loud since he was technically fresh off the farm, except his farm was more like a ranch.

"Okay, Colt, spill it," I said.

"Spill what?" he asked.

"How long have you owned that restaurant?" I asked, with a you better fess up face.

"How did you know I owned it?" Colt asked with a look of surprise on his face.

"Well, we were seated before the line that was around the block, we had the finest table in the house, the waiter knew your first name and was comfortable enough to call you that, I am pretty sure the kitchen knew what dessert you wanted before you even ordered, and lastly we didn't pay the check. So, Mr. Colt?"

"Damn, Alex, you should have been a detective instead of a designer lady!" We both laughed and Colt began to tell me all about how Cassandra had talked him into buying that place. I am sure it took some talking considering it is good ways away from the farm.

"Everything in that place, Alex, was handpicked by Cassandra. She took that and ran with it, and I have to say it is beautiful and she did an outstanding job."

"I would have to agree with you Colt. She was an amazing lady and you're right, her taste was impeccable."

We were heading back to the hotel when Colt instructed the taxi driver to take a left turn at the next light and head towards Madison Square Garden.

"In all the trips to New York, I have never had the opportunity to go to Madison Square Garden," I told Colt.

"It's beautiful at night," he said, "and there is something there for you."

"For me?" I asked. "Why would there be something there for me?" I looked at Colt like a kid waiting for Santa to come down the chimney.

"No, I am not telling you, Alex," he said as he laughed, "You will just have to wait."

Chapter 13

When we arrived at the gardens, it looked so pretty with the carriages waiting and the lights and people out walking. It looked like something out of a Norman Rockwell painting.

Colt extended his hand to help me out of the cab. "Such a gentleman," I said to him.

He tipped his hat and we had begun to walk towards the fountain, when Colt stopped and turned to me. "Alex, I want you to realize that this wasn't all my doing, but I did have a hand in it."

I looked at him with a slight smile and some confusion in my eyes. I then noticed a man walking towards us. The smile quickly left my face when I realized the surprise was Oliver. He was here in New York and walking towards me. "Colt!" I exclaimed, "Why wouldn't you tell me about this before you brought me here? Why do you have to keep surprising me with my ex-husband?"

Colt looked at me with concern and confusion in his eyes. "Ex-husband? Alex, have you made your decision?"

"I don't know yet, but Colt, why?"

At that point Oliver was standing right in front of me. "Hello Alexandra. It's nice to see you. You look beautiful as always," Oliver said softly.

"Thank you, Oliver. You're looking well too."

We stood there in awkward silence for a few seconds, and then Colt suggested we take a carriage ride. We all began to walk towards the carriages, but Colt excused himself to take a phone call.

How convenient, I thought to myself, *that Colt should get a phone call almost immediately after Oliver had walked up.*

"So," Oliver started off, "how are things with you? I heard your line went very well at the showing; you must be very excited."

"I am, Oliver. It was great! And to see our fashions up on the runway was probably the most exciting part about the entire experience! I know the merchandise that we purchased will bring in huge profits and that of course is always great, but Oliver, the feeling..." With that, I turned to him and stopped my conversation. Oliver had an excited and confused look on his face.

"Why did you stop in the middle of your sentence, Alex? You were about to tell me something else, weren't you?"

"Oliver," I asked, "why are you here? What exactly do you want from me? It seems so natural to me to just tell you everything and share my wonderful day with you, but then I realized I can't do that anymore."

"Can't or won't?" Oliver asked.

"Probably both," I said back to him. "Oliver, why are you here?"

"Alex, I know I have made a mess of things for us and I understand that you need time to sort things out, but I want you to know I love and miss you dearly. If you want to come home, I will spend the rest of my life trying to make you happy and trying to heal us."

I looked up at him with tears in my eyes and said softly, "Oliver, I would like to go back to my hotel now. I am going to grab a taxi. Would you please find Colt and tell him good night for me?"

Oliver put his hands on my shoulders and pulled me to him, and gave me the softest, most loving kiss I think we had ever exchanged. "I love you, Alex, and I am so, so sorry, but I am not ready to give up on us."

"Oliver," I stammered, "I just need to go back to the hotel."

"I will walk you to the street, Alex," and being the gentleman that he was, he hailed my cab and closed my door behind me.

On the ride back to the hotel, I could not dial Colt's number fast enough. "Voice mail? Are you kidding me Colt? Where are you, and what call was so important that you had to take it just as Oliver walked up to us? I swear Colt you better answer this phone!" I yelled. "I swear I am never going to talk to you again! You are just the most...I don't know what, but you are!" You can't really slam a cell phone down, but I hit the disconnect very hard! Now I realized Colt wouldn't know how hard I hit that button, but somehow I felt better by doing that.

When I got back to the hotel, the concierge stopped me to give me a message. I took the note from his hand and read it. Turn around, it said. I looked again at the note and turned around to see Colt standing there.

"Well. I thought you and Oliver meeting in a place as romantic as Madison Square Garden might go a little better, but, based on your message on my phone and now the look on your face, I would guess that I was wrong. Okay, Alex, let's go into the lounge and have a drink. You can yell at me there. That way I at least have a witness to my whereabouts and who I was with before I go missing!"

I stomped off to the bar and ordered a drink, not even waiting to pay the bartender when she handed it to me. Colt looked at the bartender and said, "I got this. She is a bit upset with me right now. I may need to buy several of these tonight."

Colt came over and sat down across the table from me, and before he had the chance to speak, I looked at him and asked, "Why? Why do you insist on taking Oliver's side, when even I haven't chosen sides, Colt? Why?" He opened his mouth to speak but, I cut him off again. "Why Colt? Don't you think this isn't tough enough without you sneaking around behind my back with my ex-husband and plotting something? I am so angry at you right now, Colt, that I am not really sure why I am even sitting here with you!"

"You know, Alex," Colt said softly, "That is the second time you have referred to Oliver as your ex-husband. Have you made up your mind or are you just trying to get yourself used to saying that?"

I looked at him with shock on my face. "I have called him my ex twice?" I asked. "I didn't even realize... Maybe I am...Wait, don't change the subject! This is about your actions, not mine!" I scolded.

Colt said to me, "Alex, I am not on Oliver's side or your side. I am just someone who has had two people come into my life over the past several months, and I am growing to care for both of them immensely. I realize, now, that Oliver meeting us at Madison Square Garden did not have the best outcome, but I truly was not sneaking around behind your back, and I want you to know I would not do that," Colt said in a defensive manner.

"What exactly do you call it then, Colt? If you knew, and Oliver knew, and I didn't know...why isn't that sneaking?" I asked with a tiny bit of amusement in my voice.

❤ ❤ ❤ ❤ ❤ ❤ ❤ ❤ ❤ ❤ ❤ ❤ ❤

"Okay. Well, when you put it that way Alex, it does kinda look like sneaking but...but... I am sorry Alex. I never meant to upset you. I just thought that if you and Oliver... Well, never mind what I thought; now I see it was unfair to you. I apologize, Alex. Can I get you another drink?" Colt asked.

"I am good, Colt. Thanks."

Colt went to the bar to get himself another drink, and upon returning to our table, he softly asked, "Are you ready for a divorce from Oliver?"

I looked at him and said, "I don't know yet. I know I am trying to define my life by me and not by us. Does that make any sense to you, Colt?" He shook his head yes and his eyes were filled with concern and sadness for me. "I am exhausted. Colt, I want to thank you for sharing this incredibly emotional day with me. I have been all over the charts with ups and downs, and I do believe it just caught up to me. I am going up to my room and calling it a night."

As I stood up, Colt arose as well and escorted me to the elevator. We walked to the elevator and waited for it to come to the lobby floor in silence. When the elevator doors opened, I turned to Colt and gave him a quick kiss on the cheek before stepping in to go up to my room.

Colt tipped his hat and said, "I will call you in the morning," and with that the doors closed. When I got to my room I was so exhausted that I went straight to bed. I don't think I even turned over in this large and comfortable bed until the phone rang the following morning. Kacee was on the phone and had already had way too much coffee. She was asking so many questions that my head was spinning. "Wait Kacee! Slow down! One question at a time, girl! I am not even awake yet."

"Okay, Alex, where did y'all go last night? What time did you get in? I'll wait for the answers for the first two questions before I continue on," Kacee stated. I couldn't help but laugh when she said that, and with that I sat up in bed and began to tell her how the night unfolded.

After at least an hour of telling my story, I told Kacee we needed to finish over breakfast and that I would meet her in an hour downstairs in the hotel restaurant. Just was we hung up my phone rang again, and it was Colt.

"My gosh, woman, who have you been talking to? I've been calling you for over an hour, and it went straight to voice mail each time."

"Oh, sorry, Colt, I was on the phone with Kacee."

"For over an hour?" he asked. What could you possibly have talked about for that long?"

I couldn't help but giggle and he asked, "You were talking about me, weren't you?"

"Well, isn't someone just full of themselves this morning?" We both laughed, and Colt said, "It's probably better if I don't know what you were talking about. Seriously Alex, I am sorry about Oliver and all that last night. It was out of line for me to put you in that situation."

"You know, Colt, it may have been exactly what I needed to help me decide what I was going to do. Oliver has come to me two times now and I have sent him away both times without an answer. After Kacee and I wrap up here, we are heading back home to the fashion house for a while. It's time for me to decide where I want to be. What are your plans, Colt? When does your business wrap up?"

♥ ♥ ♥ ♥ ♥ ♥ ♥ ♥ ♥ ♥ ♥ ♥

"I am almost finished here in the city as well. I have to go to a meeting tomorrow afternoon, then back to the farm for this country boy," Colt said. "I'm ready to go home and spend some time in the pink barn."

"I am sure you are. I will call you soon, Colt. Thank you for being a good friend to me!"

"Same goes for you, Alex. It's been a long time since I shared so much of my life with someone else."

As we hung up the phone, I had this overwhelming feeling that I was forgetting something. I went and enjoyed a long shower and casually dressed, put on my makeup, and packed. Then I realized what I had forgotten; Kacee. Oh crap! She was waiting for me downstairs. I finished gathering my stuff and headed out the door to find Kacee standing there.

"Oh Kacee, I am so sorry! I was on the phone with Colt and completely forgot you were waiting for me. Let's go eat breakfast; it's my treat. I am so sorry!"

"It's a continental breakfast Alex," Kacee smirked, and walked off. "And yes, I am hungry, so hurry up!" She snapped her fingers at me.

"Did you just snap your fingers?" I asked.

Kacee whirled around on me and said, "Yeah, what about it?"

"Oh nothing. Just making sure I was following directions, that's all," I said in a sugary sweet voice with the most innocent looking and pouty face I could make.

"Whatever Alex! Just keep up!"   I was practically running to keep up with her but decided it was not in my best interest to ask her if she was really so hungry that we had to run. We got to the elevator and rode down in silence. Once the doors opened, Kacee looked at me and said, "There'd better be some strawberries and waffles left, or you're in big trouble, lady."

I couldn't help but back up a little just looking at the intensity on her face. I began praying right then. *Please God please let there be waffles for this deranged woman!* I couldn't help but snicker, but was very quiet about doing so, because I wasn't sure what might possibly happen if I laughed out loud. We got our plates and thank gosh there were strawberries and waffles left for Kacee to devour. I watched her whole demeanor change as she was eating and I thought it was probably safe enough at that point to speak.

"Are your waffles good? Need more coffee?"

"No thank you, Alex," Kacee smiled. "I am fine. It's now safe to begin speaking to me again." Kacee grinned an evil grin, and we both busted out laughing. "You know you are my best friend, right Alex?"

"Yes I know that, and you are my best friend, Kacee, but why do I feel there is a but coming?"

"Well the but is: if you leave me to starve again, no one will ever find your body. Understood Alex?" Kacee asked.

"Yes, ma'am. I understand perfectly!"

"Okay, then let's go over our new product purchases as well as our timetable for delivering our new line to our clients," Kacee said.

"Sounds good," I said. "I have some projected dates for delivery. I am thinking 4 weeks."

Kacee looked up from her plate with a shocked look on her face. "That is a very short timeline, Alex. Are you sure about that?"

"I realize it is tight, but I think our personal line needs to get the exposure that it deserves, and the product we just purchased needs to be making us money. Kacee, don't you think it's time we had a raise?"

"Heck yeah!" Kacee almost shouted. "I could use some new shoes!" With that we finished our breakfast and coffee and headed to the front desk to check out.

Close to Forever, A Life Well Planned

Chapter 14

Our bags were sitting there waiting for us to gather them and we tipped the bell hop, checked out and headed for my car. I had enjoyed the drive up to the city by myself, as I had taken in the scenery and spent time clearing my head, but now I was not as excited about the drive back. I had decisions to make, both personal and professional, and wanted the opportunity to go over all of my ideas and thoughts with Kacee, but she would be on a flight back.

I looked at Kacee and said, "I didn't even ask what time your flight left. I could have made you late this morning with my lollygagging around. Or are you going to be at the airport forever? Sorry Kacee. What time do you need to be there?"

Kacee looked at me with that I am one step ahead of you look. "I canceled my flight. I am riding back with you. You don't need to go alone again, and you need me to listen to you."

I shook my head in disbelief, but at the same time I knew how well this woman knew me. "I am glad you're here Kacee. Ready to go?"

"Yes, I am very ready. I love New York, but I have missed Emy and my hubs, a lot this time," Kacee said softly.

I looked at Kacee as a smile came across her face. I used to feel that way about Oliver. Just the mention of his name, and I couldn't help but smile and think how fortunate I was. I couldn't help but tear up as these thoughts were going through my head about all the good times we had together over the years. We had seen and experienced so many things. It was almost all I could do not to break down and cry right there. What was I really going to do now? It was time to go back home, get back to work, and resume my life, but how do I do that?

Kacee looked at me as I was lost in thought and said, "So what are you going to do Alex?"

"About what?" I asked.

"You know what. You and Oliver and..." abruptly Kacee stopped her question.

"And Meghan?" I asked. "What am I going to do about my ex-husband and his daughter?"

"Ex-husband?" Kacee questioned quickly. Have you decided to divorce Oliver? Cheating rat anyway!" Kacee snapped. "Oh Alexandra, I am sorry. I should not have said that. You are my best friend, and I see the pain in you and in him, but my anger is with him, and sometimes I just want to shake him silly!"

I couldn't help but laugh at the intense look on Kacee's face. "What?" She asked. "What are you laughing at?"

"You," I snickered. "Shake him silly? That is such an old timey saying for a woman that is living the city that never sleeps and has seen just about everything this last week! Shake him silly," I laughed again.

"Whatever Alex. Whatever," she sighed with a little chuckle.

"I don't know, Kacee, what I am going to do. A part of me wants to go home, forgive him and help raise that beautiful little girl of his. But then a part of me wants to run, not walk, away from him for all the pain he has caused me. I didn't cheat on him, and I certainly didn't have a child with someone other than my spouse! I don't know if I want to deal with being a baby's momma for the next umpteen years, either. I know Oliver has gotten custody of Meghan and she will

be living with him full time. That is a lot to deal with, Kacee. I know, as a mother, you understand better than I do that kids require a lot of your time, and you give it to them because you love them and they love you, and that's how it is supposed to be. But this child is not mine; and what if I can't love her like a mom should? But, I guess I am not the mom; I am the step mom, and I didn't have a say so in this at all, Kacee. That's what I think makes me the angriest!"

Kacee listened to me for hours as we drove and took in the beautiful sites of this great country of ours. Kacee said she was getting hungry, and I knew after starving her at breakfast I'd better find something quickly for her to eat. Come to think of it, I was getting a bit hungry too. We pulled into this small diner and ordered like we were teenagers.

"I'll have the cheeseburger with fries and a small milkshake," I told the waitress.

Kacee said, "I'll have the same, except make my milkshake a large!" Kacee's eyes shone at the thought of having ice cream, even if it was in a milkshake.

"You do love your ice cream, don't you?" I laughed at Kacee. We were sitting there enjoying our meal when it dawned on me that we were only about an hour from the cabin. I needed to go by there and pick up a few of my things and make sure I had everything secured before I went back home. We finished our meal, paid the check and got into the car heading for my cabin when I thought, *I wonder if Oliver is there? Should I call him? Should I check first?*

Kacee turned and looked at me saying, "Oliver isn't at the cabin. He is at work, so don't give it another thought, Alex."

""How did you know what I am thinking sometimes, Kacee?" It's really kinda scary you know?"

"Yeah, it's a gift," Kacee smugly laughed. We drove up to the cabin and Kacee jumped out of the car like a child and ran up the stairs. "Oh, Alex, I see why you come up here! This is beautiful!"

"We haven't even been inside yet, Kacee. Wait till you see the view of the lake from the enclosed sitting porch. It is breathtaking." I opened the door and Kacee walked right in like she had been coming here all of her life.

"I love everything about this, Alex..." Kacee stopped talking in mid-sentence.

"What?" I asked. "What is it?"

"Alex, this is the most beautiful view I have ever seen; the lake, the sky, the peaceful feeling you get the second you walk in the door! It's like heaven on earth, Alex," Kacee spoke softly.

"Okay Miss Overly Dramatic, take it down a notch. It is beautiful, but it is just a cabin, not the Taj Mahal!" I laughed.

"Well, you get whatever you need to get, and I'm going to sit on the back deck and soak up the views." And with that, Kacee walked away from me like I wasn't even there.

I shook my head and went to our bedroom to gather the rest of my necessities, then to the kitchen to make sure I hadn't left anything in the fridge. It took me about an hour to take care of everything and load it in the car with no help from Kacee, who was mesmerized on the back deck and not moving for anyone. When I walked out on the deck I found Kacee asleep in the chair, and I couldn't miss the opportunity to grab the back of the rocker and pull it to me, just

Chapter 14

so I could scare her. Well it worked! Her feet went flying up in the air and her arms flailed like she was putting out a fire! I laughed so hard my stomach hurt, and I could barely catch my breath. Somehow, Kacee wasn't as amused as I was. Oh well. I think she knew I needed that, because she didn't threaten or even try to kill me.

"Get your nap out of the way, did ya, Kacee?" I asked with a slight giggle.

"Alex, I can't believe I fell asleep so quickly here! This is so restful. I would be here every weekend if I owned this place," Kacee laughed.

We have come here a lot, I thought, *but what happens now if we divorce? Do we have to sell this place? Can we share custody of the cabin?* All these thoughts began to fill my head, and I knew it was time for us to hit the road and head home. I would have to work through this, and I had to speak with Oliver.

When we reached the local store, I decided to pull in and get some snacks and gas up before we got on the expressway. As Kacee and I got out of the car, we saw Mr. Statum pumping gas. He threw his hand up and said, "Hey, Alex. Good to see you again. Tell Oliver I said hello!"

I smiled and waved back to him. "I certainly will, Mr. Statum. Good to see you, as always."

Kacee looked at me and laughed. "Do you always yell across the gravel parking lot up here?"

"Well, yes we do, as a matter of fact. That's how us mountain folk do it up here. You got a problem with that?" I asked with my best country accent.

"No problem at all," Kacee laughed and grabbed the door to the store. We got our snacks, put gas in and began the trip home.

There was a comfortable silence between Kacee and me as we drove, both of us taking in the beauty of the scenery and listening to the radio. We sang along with all the songs we knew, both of us realizing why we were in fashion and not in the music business.

After some time, Kacee leaned over and turned down the radio, looked at me and said, "Alex, you know you can stay with us for a while if you aren't sure about what your living arrangements are going to be."

I smiled at her and said, "I am going home, Kacee. It's my home and that's where I am going. I don't know what's going to happen with Oliver and me, and I don't even know how to approach anything with him, but I am going home." My voice quivered slightly as my words came out, but I knew it was inevitable that things would have to be settled.

We pulled into Kacee's driveway, and Emy came running out of the house. "Mommy, Mommy, Mommy! I have missed you so much!" She practically leapt into Kacee's arms. "What did you bring me Mommy?" Emy asked. "I know you brought me something, right, Mommy?"

"Yes, baby girl, Mommy brought you something, but you will have to help me with my luggage first. Then you can open your presents."

"Oh! Is there more than one present?" Emy squealed. "Oh, yeah!" With that, Emy jumped down and ran to me. "Hi, Aunt Alex! Did you bring me something too?"

Kacee snapped, "Emy that is not polite! Give her a hug first, then ask if she brought you anything!" We all laughed and Emy jumped into my arms.

"I love you, Aunt Alex," she said.

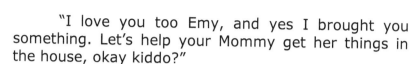

"I love you too Emy, and yes I brought you something. Let's help your Mommy get her things in the house, okay kiddo?"

"Okay, Aunt Alex." Emy ran to the other side of the car and grabbed some of the bags. "These are heavy!" Emy said. "These aren't all for me are they?" Emy asked, as her eyes widened.

"Well, most of them are, but we had to get Daddy something too you know. We don't want him to feel left out, now do we?" Kacee asked.

"No, Daddy has to have presents too," Emy said.

As we were getting the stuff out of the car, I looked at Emy and asked, "Where is your daddy? Why isn't he helping us with all of these bags?"

"Oh, he's at work. My grandma is here with me, and I just put her down for a nap. She gets kinda sleepy sometimes, and I put her to bed for a nap." Emy smiled. "Grandma says she is just resting her eyes, but I hear her snoring sometimes, so I guess her nose needs to rest too, huh Aunt Alex?"

I almost dropped the bags from laughing so hard. "I guess so Emy," I answered.

Grandma was waiting at the door. "I wasn't asleep, I was taking the cake from the oven when Emy yelled 'Mommy's home' and shot out the front door. I looked out the window and saw y'all getting out of the car, so I got my cake out. I just made some coffee if you ladies want some. Kacee, there's ice cream to go on top of your warm cake."

"Sounds good," Kacee said as she headed for the table.

"I'd better pass on the cake and coffee, but next time is a definite!" I said.

Kacee came to me and put her arms around me. "I love you Alex, and I am here if you need me."

"I know you are. Thank you, and I love you too, Kacee." I said my goodbyes and got in the car to go home.

Chapter 15

As I pulled into my driveway I could actually hear my own heart beating. I hadn't been here for several months now, and I was unsure what I was really doing here. My thoughts were exploding in my head, and I put the car in reverse to back out. *This is a mistake; I need to go to a hotel or to the fashion house. I don't need to be here yet.* I turned to look back at the house, and Oliver was standing there on the porch, just looking at me. I sat there staring at him, like I had no idea what to do next. He slowly walked over to my car and motioned for me to put the window down. I lowered the window and put the car into park and turned to look at him. We both stared at each other for a few seconds, then Meghan came running out from the back yard.

"Hi, Alex, how are you?" she asked.

"I am fine Meghan. How are you?"

"I am great! Daddy and I were just getting ready to get into the pool. Do you want to come swim with us?"

"Uh, I don't have a swimsuit honey, so I will have to do that another time," I said to her.

Her little face looked disappointed. "Okay," she said. "Daddy said he wanted to surprise you with a new pool, but it's not new. They made it yesterday. They dug a big hole and put water in it just for us, Alex!" She exclaimed.

"That's...that's great, Meghan," I stammered.

Oliver could see I was struggling and looked at Meghan. "Baby why don't you go upstairs and put on your swimsuit and get your towel. Alex and I need a minute, but do not get into the pool without me, understand?" Oliver said.

"Yes, I understand. I won't get in without you or Alex there." And with that, Meghan ran into the house.

"You put in a pool, Oliver? Wow, that's big! Um, what else have you done?"

Oliver looked at me with softness in his eyes and opened my door. "Why don't you get out and come inside?" He reached for my hand to assist me from the car as he always had done. I reached for his hand and he helped me out. He grabbed my suitcase out of the back and we walked up the sidewalk to our home. We walked silently up the stairs and Oliver opened the door for me, as he had always done.

He sat my suitcase down and turned to me, but just as he began to speak, a little voice shouted, "I'm ready to get in the pool now! Are y'all coming out here with me?"

Oliver turned to Meghan and said, "Yes, baby, we are coming right now." I stood there as Oliver headed to the back yard. When he noticed I was not walking with him, he stopped and asked me, "Alex? Are you coming?"

I motioned for him to go on and turned to walk up the stairs to our bedroom. I wanted to lay down on my big comfy bed, but when I opened the door to my room it all felt strange to me. I know Oliver had told me that they were never together in our bed, but my stomach turned to knots and I knew I couldn't be in there right now. Not yet, maybe never. *Why am I here?* I thought to myself. I walked back downstairs and realized that there was a fresh coat of paint on the walls; all of the walls. Oliver had the entire house repainted. I walked into my kitchen to realize it had

♥♥♥♥♥♥♥♥♥♥♥♥♥♥

been totally redone. All new appliances, new cabinets, new flooring, and new lighting. It all looked amazing. Oliver had impeccable taste, and he had outdone himself.

I watched from the kitchen window as Meghan played in the pool. She truly was a beautiful child, and her laughter filled the yard. I stood there for quite some time watching Oliver as he watched his daughter very closely. I heard her squeal, "Get in with me Daddy! Get in and play with me! Where is Alex?" she asked. "Isn't she coming to play in our new pool with us, Daddy?"

Oliver looked back towards the window and saw me standing there staring at him. He looked back at his little girl and said, "I don't know baby. Maybe we need to let her get settled in. She's had a long drive home today."

"Okay Daddy," Meghan said, then went back to splashing in the water.

I looked at the clock and realized it was dinner time and I was hungry. I grabbed an apple and walked out to the back yard where Oliver and Meghan were now playing on the swing.

"Oh, Alex, will you come and swing me please?" Meghan asked. I walked slowly over to her and began to push her in the swing. "Higher! Higher, Alex!" she squealed! Her laughter was contagious and I couldn't help but laugh with her. After some time on the swing, Meghan looked at me and said she was hungry and wanted to know if we could have roasted marshmallows for supper. I couldn't help but laugh at her request. With that, Oliver stepped over and stopped the swing. "Meghan, it's time for you to go wash your hands and get ready for supper."

♥♥♥♥♥♥♥♥♥♥♥♥♥♥

"Okay Daddy, but can we have marshmallows?" she asked with such happiness in her little eyes.

Oliver laughed, "Not for supper, but later tonight we will. Now go wash your hands." With that Meghan ran off to her bathroom to wash up. Oliver looked at me and said, "Looks like you two were having fun out here. Come on Alex, I have dinner ready for us."

I guess I lost track of time pushing Meghan on the swing, and didn't even realize that Oliver had gone inside and fixed our dinner for us. As we were walking to the house Oliver reached to hold my hand. I guess the look in my eyes said it all, because he pulled his hand back, smiled and said to me, "When you are ready, Alex."

We went into the kitchen and sat down to eat our dinner. Meghan reminded us that we needed to say grace before we started. She also said we kinda needed to hurry, because she was really hungry. We both laughed and bowed our heads to pray. Meghan said, "God thank you for this good supper my daddy fixed, thank you for my new pool, and my Barbie beach towel, and thank you God for bringing Alex home. Amen." Then she and handed her plate to her father.

I saw the smile on Oliver's face, knowing he was thinking that he had his family with him and everything was going to work out. I looked at him and said, "I don't know if it will." The smile left his face and his eyes saddened.

"You knew what I was thinking, Alex. You have always been able to read me, just like I can read you. I will spend the rest of my life doing my very best to make you happy and to ease the pain that I have caused you."

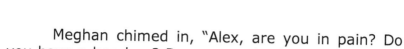

Meghan chimed in, "Alex, are you in pain? Do you have a boo boo? Do you need a band aid? I have some Barbie band aids in my bathroom. I can go get you one!"

"Meghan, that is so sweet of you. Thank you, but I am fine," I told her, looking into her little face.

"Okay," Meghan said, "but if you decide you do want one, I will share mine with you." Meghan looked at me and said, "I'm finished eating. I want to go to my room and play. I nodded my head and she ran up the stairs.

I glanced over to Oliver; he had the most peaceful look on his face with a smile from ear to ear. "Oliver, what are you smiling at?" I asked.

He looked at me and said softly, "This is right for us Alex. This all fits. Tonight we sat together as a family in our home with our child, eating dinner. This is what my life is supposed to be, Alex."

He was about to say something else when I held my hand up to him. "Oliver," I softly whispered his name, "please don't say any more. I know you feel this will all be okay, but I am just trying to decide if I am even staying here tonight or going to the fashion house apartment."

The look on Oliver's face was one of shock and sadness. "I thought you were coming home to make this work out, Alex. I wasn't even sure you would walk through our front door, but then you came in, watched Meghan play, ate dinner with us...I know this will all come together for us, Alex and we will be great again," Oliver said with such confidence in his voice.

I looked at him and remembered that was one of the things I loved so much about him; his complete devotion to something when he felt it was right in his heart. "Oliver, let me explain some things to you," I snipped. "I think your daughter is a beautiful child and I know you are a great father. I also know that Meghan being here is exactly what you want and need. I have to give credit to Ellen for allowing this. She must have realized more quickly than I did how desperately you wanted a child. I cannot fully grasp the fact that she has allowed her child to live with you, but that is not mine to deal with."

Oliver looked at me and smiled softly. "I understand, Alex. This is a lot for you to try to absorb. I keep telling myself that if you just spend some time around Meghan, you will fall in love with her too. As far as Ellen goes, Alex, no one will understand me as well as you do. You know what I am thinking, what I am feeling and what I am striving for. You always have."

Oliver reached over and put his hand on mine, and at that moment I saw another reason why I loved him so much. I pulled my hand away from his touch and slid my chair out from the table. Suddenly, we heard a loud thud and a piercing scream coming from the stairway.

Chapter 16

Oliver sprang to his feet and ran to towards the scream. "Meghan!" Oliver shouted. My heart leapt into my throat as I followed behind Oliver. When we reached Meghan she was crying and pointing at her foot. Oliver knelt on the floor beside her, inspecting her foot and asking her where it hurt.

I knelt down beside her, and in a calm voice said to her, "Meghan, you are okay baby girl? You just need to tell us where you hurt." I looked into her eyes and saw the fear and pain that she was in. "Breathe just like me Meghan, just like me," I said, and we both began to breathe more slowly together. "Okay sweetie, show me where it hurts," I said to her.

Meghan pointed at her ankle and said, "I jumped off the steps and my ankle landed before my foot did, Alex. It hurts really bad. Please make it stop hurting!"

I looked her in the eye and told her I would make the pain go away. I looked at Oliver, who was staring at the both of us and said, "Daddy, pick her up and take her to the car. We need to go to the hospital to get this looked at." Oliver picked up Meghan and started towards the car without hesitation. I grabbed my purse and my keys and headed to the car.

Oliver was a nervous wreck, and I realized I needed to drive us there. Oliver buckled Meghan in and slid in beside her, constantly reassuring her that he was there, and she was going to be okay.

Meghan looked at Oliver and said, "Daddy, Alex is going to make the pain go away, but I sure hope she hurries. This really hurts!"

I looked at Oliver in the mirror and saw him looking at me. We both kinda chuckled at what Meghan had said, and he assured her that Alex would make the pain go away as quickly as she could.

When we reached the hospital, the pediatric doctor was waiting for us. I had called on the way out the door and told them that we were on our way with Meghan, that she had hurt her ankle and we would be there within minutes. The nurse asked Meghan if she would come with her in the wagon and Meghan nodded her head yes, but would not let go of Oliver's hand. Oliver looked at me and I shook my head yes, I knew he needed to be with her and I reached for the clipboard to fill out the insurance papers.

"Alex," Meghan cried out, "aren't you coming too?"

"Yes Meghan, I am coming too. I just have to do this really quickly and then I will be right beside you, okay?"

"Okay Alex," Meghan sniffled, and they went behind the double doors to the exam room. I began filling out the paperwork—all the basics; name, address, phone, insurance carrier, but when I got to the relationship, I realized I wasn't related to this child. I wasn't sure what to put down in that box. That little box brought me to a stop. In the moments getting her here and calming her down, I felt like a mom, but then in black and white, in a box on a paper, I was nothing to this little girl. Anger flew through me and I almost put the clipboard down and walked away. This was not mine to handle!

Oliver, I thought, *this is all your fault! I did nothing wrong, and Meghan certainly did nothing wrong!* I skipped the box and continued onward. All the rest was easy, and when I handed the paperwork

♥♥♥♥♥♥♥♥♥♥♥♥♥♥♥♥

to the nurse, she quickly went over the cost with me and told me I had missed a box, the one that said relationship. I looked at the nurse and told her, "This little girl is my husband's child." Tears began to fill my eyes.

"I understand," she said, with a look of sadness for me. "They are in ER bay 21. Just follow the red line on the floor." With that, she opened the door for me to go in. As I reached bay 21 I could hear Meghan and Oliver giggling and I couldn't help but giggle too. She truly is a beautiful child inside and out, and I smiled as I walked into the room.

"Alex!" Meghan squealed, like she hadn't seen me in months.

I smiled at her and said, "Hey Meghan; how are you feeling?"

"Oh, Alex, the doctor took me to get my ankle's picture taken, but I don't think it smiled like I do when I get my picture taken."

"Why do you think your ankle didn't smile, Meghan?" I asked her.

"I don't know," she said softly and closed her eyes.

Oliver looked at me and whispered, "They had to give her some medicine for the pain, but nothing is broken."

"I am very relieved to hear that, Oliver. Are they letting her go home now?" I asked.

"Yes," he said and rose to come to me. He reached out his hand and put it on my shoulder. "I am glad you were here, Alex. You kept her calm and knew what to do, just like a mother would know." I looked at him and the tears began to fall down my cheek. "Alex?" he asked, "Why are you crying? Meghan is going to be fine. The doctor said it's just a sprain."

Just as I began to speak the nurse came in and informed us that she had Meghan's discharge papers completed and we could go home now. Oliver reached over and picked up Meghan, who didn't stir too much, and we walked to the car to take her home. Once she was fastened in her car seat, Oliver got in the back to ride beside her and I drove us home.

As we reached our house, Oliver unbuckled Meghan and went to pick her up. She looked at me and asked if I would carry her into the house. I nodded my head yes, and reached to put her into my arms. When Oliver looked at me with that my life is complete smile, the anger flashed in my eyes and he quickly stepped back.

Oliver unlocked the door and I carried Meghan to her room where she went back to sleep quickly. Oliver was standing behind me, and when I turned around to leave Meghan's room, the confusion on his face spoke volumes.

"You have no idea, do you Oliver? No idea at all!" I had to stop myself from shouting at him as I walked past him and headed downstairs.

Oliver quietly closed Meghan's door and followed me down the stairs. "Alex, why are you upset? Why do you have your keys in your hand? Aren't you staying here at home with your family tonight?" Oliver asked with confusion and annoyance in his voice.

I turned around so aggressively that Oliver took a step back from me. I looked at him and said, "Don't you dare take that tone with me Oliver! Don't you dare! Why am I upset? I will tell you why I am upset. As you were back in the room with Meghan and I was filling out the insurance papers, it asked me what relation I was to the patient. Guess what Oliver! I am not related to the patient at all! Don't you dare, Oliver! You have been so unfair, and I am just supposed to forgive and forget all of this because you feel completed by having your daughter and your wife in the same house? Well you may be complete, Oliver, but I am far from that! I am torn in a million pieces and it's all because you didn't take our vows seriously! You committed adultery, not me! Don't you dare think this is all okay, because it is not!" I seethed with anger and I shook with the fury that was once again inside me. "Then you have the audacity to try and put guilt on me by asking why I am not staying in our home with our family tonight! Shame on you Oliver!" I snapped.

"Alexandra, I know that everything isn't perfect, but if you keep running away, how is it going to be anywhere close to right again?" Oliver stepped cautiously towards me and put his hand out for mine. "Alex, my list of what I should have done keeps growing and I don't know if I know what to do either. I want this to work out and I want us to be a happy family. I am sorry I cheated on you, and I am not sure you will ever be able to forgive me. Right now, I am unsure of how to fix anything. I know I have a daughter that I love with all my heart, and I have a wife that I love with all my heart, and I have made a mess of everything!" With that, Oliver slid down the wall and began to sob like a broken man.

"Oliver," I said softly, "I am not sure what to do either. I am so sorry I couldn't give you a child. I am sorry that Meghan is not mine. She is a beautiful little girl and I would no doubt fall in love with her. I am trying to handle all of this, but it is so difficult."

Oliver shook his head without lifting it. "I know it is," he whispered.

A part of me wanted to reach out and hold him, while a part of me wanted to yell at him. *You did this; you caused the break in our home. This is all on you!*

I stood there staring at him for a few minutes. Then I heard Meghan call for me. "Alex? Are you here?" Meghan asked quietly.

"Yes, Meghan, I am here. "Do you need something?" I asked.

"I want a drink of water, please."

"Okay, I'm getting it. "You get back into bed and I will be right up, okay?"

"Okay Alex, I will," she said, and I heard her footsteps as she walked back to her room.

I went to the kitchen to get her water when I saw that Oliver had gotten up from the floor and was trying to compose himself as he reached for the glass. "No, I've got this," I said softly as I shook my head. "Why don't you go freshen up and make us some tea? I would love some cinnamon and orange zest in mine," I said as I walked up the stairs to Meghan's room.

Meghan was sitting there in her bed waiting for her water with her eyes about half way open. I handed her the glass and she took a very small drink, and then snuggled back into her comforter. I sat down on the bed beside her and she reached her hand towards me. I put her hand in mine and sat there watching her sleep. I really did feel connected to this precious child. I was just not sure what to do with her father. I had so much anger and felt so betrayed by him. I didn't know how to process the anger. Then I looked at his adorable child with her big heart, bright eyes, and the most contagious laugh in the world. I was saddened that she was not my daughter. I hadn't even been around her that much and I already knew she was going to be a very big part of my life. "I'm not sure

how all of this is going to work, Meghan, but I promise to be there for you always."

Meghan turned to me, opened her little eyes and said softly, "I love you, Alex."

I stroked her hair and whispered, "Get some sleep. I will check on you later." I turned on her Barbie night light and closed her door on my way downstairs.

Oliver was sitting on the couch when I walked into the room, and my tea was waiting for me beside his. "I'll warm it back up for you, Alex. I'm sure it has cooled off considerably by now," Oliver said as he began to rise to his feet.

"Its fine, Oliver. Really, don't bother. I sat down and reached for my tea and took a sip. "It's still pretty warm," I said with a small smile on my face.

"Did Meghan go back to sleep?" Oliver asked.

"She is fine, Oliver. She just needs to rest for a while."

I looked at Oliver and smiled. "Well, this certainly has been a busy day now, hasn't it?"

He looked at me and shook his head. "Alex, if you want to go to the fashion house, I will understand. Don't get me wrong. I want you here with us, but I do understand."

I set my tea down, turned to Oliver and said, "Your daughter just told me she loves me. I'm going to get a shower and go to bed. I'll see you in the morning. And yes, you are sleeping in the guest room." With that, I got up and went upstairs to bed. I don't know how long Oliver sat there staring at me as I walked away, but I know the shock on his face was enough to make me giggle a bit. I climbed the stairs, not really sure what I was feeling or even doing, but I did know I was tired and this was my house and I was ready to call it a night. I opened Meghan's door slightly to check on her and she was sound asleep with the most angelic look on her face. That little girl was so unexpected in my world and yet I knew in my heart that good was going to come out of all of this.

I closed her door and walked down the hallway towards mine and Oliver's bedroom. As I reached for the doorknob, this overwhelming feeling flooded over me. Except for gathering a few of my things, I had not been back in our bedroom since I found out about Oliver's infidelity and the events that had now changed our lives. I walked over to our bed and sat down on the corner. Maybe I couldn't sleep in here; maybe this wasn't a good idea at all. Maybe I needed to just gather some of my belongings and go to the fashion house or a hotel.

As I sat there lost deep in thought, Oliver knocked on the door and asked, "Can I come in?" I looked at him and nodded my head yes. He walked over to me and sat down beside me on the bed. He didn't speak a word, just placed his hand on mine and sat there.

I don't know how long we sat there, but when I turned to him and looked deeply into his eyes, my voice cracked as I began to speak. "Oliver, it feels like forever since we..."

Before I could say another word, the phone rang. I reached to answer it, but Oliver stopped me.

"Alex, let it ring. Finish what you were going to say."

"Oliver, what I was going to say was, I... why isn't the answering machine picking up?"

Oliver looked at me with a confused look on his face. "You were going to ask me why the answering machine isn't picking up?"

"No, Oliver! Answer the phone please," I told him.

He grabbed the phone and practically yelled, "Hello!"

I could hear Kacee's voice screaming through the phone, "Where is Alex? Oliver, I need to talk to her now!"

"Kacee, what is it?" Oliver asked. "Okay, here she is."

Chapter 17

Oliver handed me the phone, but Kacee was talking too loud and so fast that I was having difficulty understanding her. "Wait, Kacee...your house caught fire? Kacee, slow down! I can't understand what you're saying. Is everyone okay? What? What? Kacee!" I screamed, "Now stop this yelling and tell me what is happening. Stop it now Kacee!" With that, Kacee caught her breath and told me the horrible news that the fashion house was on fire. "Kacee, I am on my way!" I hung up, ran downstairs to get my purse and keys, and got ready to rush to the fashion house. Oliver was calling my name but I didn't stop to answer him. I yelled out, "I have to go!" and with that I had my keys in hand and ran to my car.

I flew out of the driveway, hoping to get there in time to do something, to save something. I don't know what I was thinking, really, I just knew that I needed to see what was happening. I got to the barricades and jumped from my car. The policeman standing there tried to grab me, but I ran past him with ease. He yelled after me to stop, but I continued on.

I did not, however, make it past the next officer standing there. I didn't even see the officer who stopped me; it was just like my body was circling in the air before I could realize he had caught me. "Ma'am? Ma'am? You can't go in there. It's a total loss." I tried to free myself from his grip but he was not letting me go.

"Officer, you don't understand. That is my world right there. Please let me go! Please, I have to get my designs! They're burning up in there! And I have too many years invested in this house! Please!" I exclaimed.

The officer tightened his arms around me, and I knew he was not going to let me go. I began to sob, and at that point the officer loosened his grip on me. I guess he realized at that point that I understood I had no choice but to watch in horror as my career literally went up in flames.

He whispered in my ear, "I am sorry," and with that unlocked his arms from around me and let me go. I stood there staring, watching a war of flames versus water hoses, and at that point I didn't care which one would win. I just knew I had lost!

I heard Kacee calling my name, and I turned to see where she was. She walked slowly up to me and we put our arms around each other. We just stood there. I don't know how long it took to get the flames out, but it seemed like forever. All we could do was just stand there.

The fire marshal came over and said, "It looks like the fire started in the finishing room. Looks like there was a design iron left on." I looked at him with a blank look on my face, and he told me the official report would be ready in 2 days and I could pick it up then. "Ma'am, I am sorry," he said, and handed me his business card. "If you need anything, my number is right there," he said, and with that, he turned around and yelled to the firemen, "Let's wrap it up boys!"

As the fire department was leaving and the crowd that had gathered dispersed, Kacee and I stood there in disbelief at what had happened in the last 4 hours. Once again, the tears began to stream down my face. I looked at Kacee and she was expressionless, with just a blank look on her face. I took her hand in mine and said, "Let's go get some

❤ ❤ ❤ ❤ ❤ ❤ ❤ ❤ ❤ ❤ ❤ ❤

breakfast. Today is going to be a very busy day for us." Kacee didn't speak a word, just held my hand, and we walked to the diner around the corner.

It was now early morning and as we sat there at the diner waiting for our food to arrive, neither of us could find any words to say. It was just a silence that spoke louder than any words. The waitress brought our coffee, and at that moment I saw Oliver looking through the window with his face pressed against the glass. When I saw that, I started laughing out loud. Kacee looked at me like I was half out of my mind, which I am sure I was, but then Oliver walked through the door. I laughed louder and louder until people began to stare. Kacee still had not seen Oliver at this point and asked me if I needed her to call my doctor.

Oliver slid in beside me in the booth, and Kacee looked at me with that very confused look on her face. He put his arm around me and whispered, "I am so sorry, love. I tried calling you a million times last night but you didn't answer the phone." "I saw on the news this morning that the building was in flames. I would have come with you, but Meghan was asleep, and I didn't know what had happened and..."

"Oliver, it's okay," I said, "I understand. How did Meghan sleep last night? Wait...where is she? Who is watching Meghan?" I asked with almost panic in my voice.

"She slept fine," Oliver said, "And I asked Mrs. Sigel to watch over her for a little while."

Oh, okay good." Mrs. Sigel had been our next-door neighbor since we bought the house. She was a wonderful lady who had lost her husband last year. She loved spending time with her own grandchildren and with the neighborhood kids.

♥ ♥ ♥ ♥ ♥ ♥ ♥ ♥ ♥ ♥ ♥ ♥

"Alex, Kacee, you both look exhausted. Why don't you both go home and get some rest?" Oliver suggested.

"Are you kidding me?" I snapped. "We have so much work to do, and our day will be a long one, so we need to get started! Kacee, we need to get finished here and get going," I said in a determined voice. "Okay," Kacee said, "Where are we going and what are we doing?"

"We need to contact the staff and let them all know what's going on; we need to contact a real estate agent to find us a new factory to work in; and, most importantly, contact our clients and assure them that their products will be ready and delivered on time."

Kacee looked at me with excitement in her eyes, knowing we were going to get us back on track, and very soon. Oliver looked at me and grabbed the ticket to go pay for our breakfast as my phone rang. It was Mr. Elwin on the phone. Mr. Elwin was the owner of the fashion house, and even though I had been in charge of all aspects of running the business, I still had a boss of my own. Mr. Elwin was a very sweet older man who had lost interest in the day to day running of the fashion house since his wife had passed away. He was calling to make sure all of us were okay.

"We are all fine sir. No one was in the building at the time of the fire. The official report from the fire department will be ready in a couple of days, and we can decide on our plan at that time, sir," I said.

Then I was taken aback as Mr. Elwin told me that he would not be reopening this fashion house and would sell me the name and all rights if I were interested. He explained that he was getting older and had made a very comfortable life, but no longer

124

wanted to have anything that would tie him here. He wanted to move to Florida and live the rest of his life near his children.

Chapter 18

Mr. Elwin asked if I would like to purchase Excellence Fashion House from him, and before he finished his question, I said, "Yes, yes, I want to purchase the name and all rights to this fashion name."

The company was built by Mr. Elwin and his late wife, but in all honesty this man and this fashion house helped to build me. I was saddened and excited at the same time. I was now going to own a fashion name that was established and had a very strong reputation in the fashion industry. I realized that putting out our first line this year was a little new for us, but the reviews were exceptional and the profits were already exceeding expectations. I thanked Mr. Elwin and hung up the phone.

Kacee and Oliver were staring at me when I blurted out, "I am now the owner of Excellence Fashion House and Designs! Mr. Elwin just told me he is selling everything to me and that we would meet with the attorneys in the morning to get the ball rolling. Oh Oliver, I am so excited!" I squealed.

Kacee and I looked at each other and at the same time said, "We really are going to be busy now!" Both of us laughed and we headed outside.

Oliver reached to open the door for us and once we walked through, he turned to me and said, "I am going home to check on Meghan." Then, he quietly walked away. Kacee looked at me with a confused look on her face, and I shrugged my shoulders and we walked to my car.

Chapter 19

After a full day and evening of putting things in order, it was time to go home. I dropped Kacee off at her car and instructed her to call our employees and give them the address of the new location and what time to be there in the morning to begin working.

During the short drive home, my mind was racing with new and old ideas, thoughts, and plans. This was going to be quite an adventure. I was almost too excited to concentrate on my whereabouts, and actually missed the driveway to my own home. I had to circle the block and make myself focus on where to turn. I pulled into the driveway, continued the conversation that I had been having with myself all the way home, and grabbed my stuff out of the car. I realized everything in my life was falling back into place and it was all starting to feel right again. "Okay," I said out loud, "There will be much work ahead, but right now it was time to get in a hot bath, have a glass of wine and try to relax." I couldn't help but giggle when the word relax came out of my mouth. *That actually went through my head? And I actually said it? Me, relax? Too funny Alex!*

I opened the door and smelled an amazing scent coming from the kitchen. It was then that I realized I was starving since I hadn't eaten since very early this morning. Oliver was standing by the stove and Meghan was helping to set the table for dinner.

I stood there looking at the both of them with a comfortable smile on my face when Meghan said, "Alex, you need to go change into your comfy clothes and come eat dinner with me and Daddy."

I nodded my head yes and went upstairs to get changed. I could hear Oliver and Meghan laughing in the kitchen and I couldn't help but smile and giggle with them. I got changed and went back downstairs where the two of them were waiting for me at the table. I joined them and Oliver reached for my hand as we bowed our heads to ask the blessing.

It had always been a tradition for Oliver and me to add our daily thoughts to our prayers, so I wasn't surprised when Meghan began to add her daily thoughts. "God, thank you for my daddy, and my new swing, and I love spaghetti with meatballs and, God, if Alex doesn't mind, can I start calling her Mommy? Amen!" Meghan said.

I raised my eyes to this precious child and was overwhelmed with emotion and love for her. I nodded my head yes and whispered softly to Meghan, "Is it okay for me to call you my daughter?"

Meghan whispered softly, "Yes, Mommy."

I looked over at Oliver, and his eyes were full of emotion and tears. We both smiled at each other and began to eat the most amazing spaghetti I had ever tasted. Maybe it was the food; maybe it was the fact that yet another time today I had the feeling in my heart that everything was going to be okay in my world. We sat there and ate dinner, talked about our day, and just enjoyed the three of us being together.

As we finished our meal and began to clear the dishes from the table, Meghan handed me her plate and asked if she could help load the dishwasher. I couldn't help but snicker because growing up, one of my least favorite jobs was loading and unloading the dishwasher, and this little child want to help.

"Yes, you can, Meghan." We went over where the glasses, plates, pans, and silverware had to go,

Chapter 19

♥ ♥ ♥ ♥ ♥ ♥ ♥ ♥ ♥ ♥ ♥ ♥

and how much detergent needed to be added, and where it had to be added. I stood there in amazement of this child and how incredibly smart she was.

As we cleaned the kitchen, we discussed her little world, and I realized we needed to get her prepared for kindergarten, and school in general. Meghan would be going to school in the fall, and it was time to get her registered, buy her clothes, get her school supplies, and do what parents do to get their child ready for this new adventure.

"Meghan, will you go get your daddy while I finish the kitchen? I need to talk to him please."

"Sure mommy, I will go get him," and Meghan scurried away yelling throughout the house, "Daddy, Mommy wants you."

I couldn't help but smile when I heard those words and repeated them to myself. *Daddy, Mommy wants you.*

Oliver came into the kitchen as I was making some coffee. "Need any help in here Alex?"

"Good timing," I smirked, "We just finished cleaning up. I do want to talk, Oliver. Please sit down with me."

"Of course," he said as he grabbed the coffee cups from the cupboard.

"Where is Meghan?" I asked him.

"She is watching TV in the den. Alex, are you okay?" he asked.

"I am fine, Oliver, but I think it is time we speak to an attorney."

"Attorney?" Oliver asked as his voice cracked.

"Yes, Oliver, the time has come, and I think we need to make everything official and legal. It's what's best for Meghan," I said softly.

"Oh Alex, I am so sorry. Please give me time. Everything seems to be falling into place so perfectly, so please don't file for divorce. I love you with all that I am and I don't want to lose you."

Oliver opened his mouth to speak again, and I couldn't help but snicker, "Oliver, stop talking...I want to be Meghan's legal mother. I need to adopt her, so she is legally my own child and I am legally her mommy. There are many things that will come up for us over the years and I need to legally be able to make decisions, and sign permission slips for school activities, and so forth. Please call Perry and make an appointment for us to go forward with me adopting Meghan."

I don't think I had even finished my sentence when Oliver was dialing the phone for Perry. I went over to refill our coffee cups and heard Oliver say, "Thanks, Perry, we will see you in the morning." Oliver put the phone down, came to me and put his arms around me. There were tears in both of our eyes when Oliver whispered in my ear, "I love you so much, Alex. Thank you."

"I love you too, Oliver, and our daughter."

Oliver leaned in gently to kiss me, and without resistance I kissed him as well. It had been a long struggle to get to this point, but I knew in my heart that he was the man I loved and Meghan was the daughter I was supposed to have.

"We need to go tell Meghan what's going to happen," I said to Oliver, so hand in hand we went to the den to share the good news with her.

Meghan was watching her favorite show, which was about over when she stopped and looked at us. "You two are holding hands she said, just like really mommies and daddies do. That's pretty cool," Meghan

Chapter 19

♥ ♥ ♥ ♥ ♥ ♥ ♥ ♥ ♥ ♥ ♥ ♥ ♥

said softly as she turned back to watch the rest of her show.

I stood there looking down at this child in total amazement of what she picked up on and understood. Sometimes I think she could teach her father and me something about growing up. I laughed to myself. When Meghan's show was over, she turned to me and asked why we were staring at her.

"I am just happy to have you in my life. Meghan, your father and I want to talk to you about something very important."

"Okay," she said, "What's up?" I stood there hoping the words would come to me and make sense of what I was trying to tell her, but I couldn't even start. Then Oliver began to speak. "Meghan, you know that Mommy didn't give birth to you..."

"I know Daddy, Ellen did."

"That's right baby, Ellen did, but since Mommy didn't, there are some papers that will need to be completed by our lawyer to make Alex legally your mommy." Oliver knelt down by Meghan and asked, "Do you understand what we are talking about so far, sweetie?"

Meghan nodded her head yes and looked at me. "Alex is going to adopted me."

I knelt down as well and held her little hand. "Yes, Meghan, I am going to adopt you, if you would like me to."

Meghan put her arms around my neck and said, "I really want you to, but does that mean my name has to change?"

I looked at her with a quizzical look. "Why do you think your name would have to change?" I asked her.

"Well, when people on the TV get adopted, they have to change their name, and I like my name being Meghan."

Oliver and I looked at each other, then to Meghan and laughed. "No, baby, your name won't change. It will stay Meghan."

"I am glad. I have gotten very used to it," Meghan stated, as she turned back to watch some more TV.

I looked over at Oliver, and he winked at me with a smile on his face from ear to ear. We left Meghan very engrossed in her show and went to the kitchen to finish our coffee. Oliver took my hand and squeezed it, then turned and kissed my cheek and told me how lucky a man he was.

I snickered and shook my head, and then said to him, "Yes, you are a very lucky man!" I picked up my coffee and realized it had gotten cold in the time we were in the other room, so I poured it out and headed to my office to work on some ideas for the new fashion house.

I soon heard Oliver and Meghan laughing together in the den as they watched their favorite cartoon. Oliver had told me on many occasions it was Meghan's favorite, but I had the feeling he loved it as much as she did. After a few hours of designs, numbers, and spreadsheets, I ready for a break, so I called to Meghan that it was time for her bath and bed. We had a big day tomorrow and we all needed to be on top of our game.

Meghan scurried off to get her jammies and get ready for her bath. Oliver was getting the bath ready when I got to the bathroom. He really was a good father and I was seeing that this would all work out.

Chapter 19

♥ ♥ ♥ ♥ ♥ ♥ ♥ ♥ ♥ ♥ ♥ ♥ ♥

We already were a family but needed to tie up some loose ends and make everything legal.

I smiled at Oliver and had gone to turn down Meghan's bed when I heard a loud squeal as Meghan jumped into the tub. After she had played awhile and gotten clean, it was time for night-night. I read her a bedtime story and Meghan soon drifted off to sleep. It really was a perfect day in our world and I was feeling very blessed to be a part of this. I turned off Meghan's night light and walked out her door to find Oliver standing there in the hall waiting for me. I looked at him and he smiled the softest smile.

"Yes?" I asked. "Why are you looking at me like that?"

Chapter 20

Oliver took my hand, led me into our bedroom, and quietly closed the door behind us. It had been quite a long time since we had been in our room together. Oliver gently pulled me to him and kissed me like we were on our first date. I have to admit a part of me wanted to back up and leave, but the bigger part of me had missed my husband and truly was ready to let myself become one with him again.

I have to admit that I was somewhat nervous because so much time had passed, and so much had happened, that I wasn't sure what to expect of myself or him.

Oliver saw the caution in my eyes and softly whispered to me, "We will only go where you are comfortable, Alex."

After hearing those words, I felt a wave come over me that washed the hardness that I had been keeping in my heart away. Oliver and I enjoyed a beautiful night together, and I have to admit that was probably the best sleep I had in a long time.

I woke up to Oliver looking at me and stroking my hair. I smiled at him and asked, "Why are you looking at me like that again?"

He leaned down and kissed me and whispered, "Because I am the luckiest man in the world!" and with that we both laughed.

I knew we had an appointment with Perry this morning, and I knew if we were going to be there on time I was going to have to get us up and going. "Oliver, will you call Mrs. Sigel and see if she can watch Meghan for us while we meet with Perry this morning?" I asked.

"I already did, and she said she would love to keep Meghan," he replied.

"Excellent!" I said as I looked at the clock. "Oh, we are going to be late, Oliver. Why did you let me sleep in so late?" We both knew that was a rhetorical question and I hurriedly made my way to the shower.

I rushed through my shower and tried to get dressed as quickly as possible so that I could get Meghan up and ready to go, but to my surprise she was already dressed and putting her shoes on when I went into her room.

"Good morning, Mommy," she said so matter of factly that I couldn't help but smile the biggest smile at her.

"Good morning baby girl. Are you ready to go see Mrs. Sigel today?" I asked.

"Oh yes! I love working in her flower garden with her. She lets me pull the weeds and water the flowers with her."

I stood there in total amazement of this child. She is so incredibly smart and is always ready for an adventure. "Okay, then. We don't need to keep Mrs. Sigel waiting, do we now?"

Meghan scurried down the stairs where Oliver was waiting for us. "Good morning Daddy," Meghan said as she ran by him to the refrigerator to get her chocolate milk.

"Good morning, Princess," Oliver laughed and shouted, since Meghan was already gone from his sight. Then as he turned to hand me my coffee, Meghan was there between us. "Wow! You are fast little girl," Oliver exclaimed.

"It's a big day Daddy! You and Mommy have to go see the lawyer, and I have to go have breakfast

with Mrs. Sigel and work in the garden. We need to go, right, Mommy?" Meghan asked.

"Yes, yes, we do need to go," I said with a smile on my face.

Mrs. Sigel was waiting on the porch for Meghan, and they both hugged each other, waved bye to Oliver and me, and went inside.

Oliver and I just kinda stood there staring at each other. Then he said to me, "Well, guess we better go huh?" We both laughed and got in the car.

Chapter 21

The ride to Perry's office seemed to take forever. I wanted this to get moving quickly so I could legally adopt Meghan and move forward with raising our daughter. I reached over and squeezed Oliver's hand, and he looked at me with the most peaceful and happy expression on his face. It was nice to see him like this again, and it was nice to feel this way again.

"Our life is back on track, Oliver," I said.

We pulled into the parking garage of Perry's office, and as I was getting ready to open my door, Oliver turned my face to his, and with almost fear in his eyes asked me, "Have you forgiven me, Alex?"

The question hit me like a brick wall, and I wasn't sure exactly how to answer, so I didn't. I smiled at him and got out of the car.

We walked into Perry's office and his secretary took us straight back to him. Perry stood up and shook Oliver's and my hands. "Good to see you both! How are ya?" he asked. Perry extended his hand for us to sit down and asked, "So why are y'all here?"

We had been friends with Perry and his family for years. His wife Evelyn worked at the local library and their three kids were well behaved and very active in their school events. Perry knew we didn't have children, but we had talked to him about the possibility of adoption a while ago. However, the town we live in is not a huge city, so word gets around. Perry was aware that there was a child somewhere in the picture now.

"Perry," Oliver began, "I have a—well we have a..." and at that point Oliver looked at me as though the words would not come out of his mouth.

I put my hand on Oliver's, and with a reassuring look began to speak. "Perry," I said, "We have a daughter that is not biologically mine, and I want to adopt her. Oliver is her biological father and his name is on the birth certificate, but now I need my name on there as well. Ellen is the birth mom and has her own family and has decided not to be active in Meghan's life. Ellen and her husband are in agreement about this, so what do you need to do to make this legal?"

Perry smiled, "That's what I like about you, Alex. You are just a straight to the point kind of person."

"Well thank you, Perry, I think!" and we both laughed.

"Oliver, Alex, if this is as cut and dried as you portray, then we shouldn't have any obstacles to jump over. Hopefully the longest part will be getting it on the judge's docket."

Excellent! I thought to myself.

"Oliver," Perry asked, "Do you have Ellen's number?"

"Yes, I do," he answered quickly, and gave it to him.

Perry wasted no time calling Ellen, and to our surprise she answered on the first ring. Perry introduced himself and explained that he was representing us for the adoption of Meghan by Alexandra. Ellen was very soft-spoken on the phone. She explained that her kids were in the next room playing and she didn't want them to overhear our conversation. Perry assured her we understood and asked if she were prepared to relinquish her parental rights to Meghan and allow Alex to adopt her. There was a pause on the phone, and for that instant I felt my heart beat so hard I truly thought it would come

out of my chest, but then Ellen said softly, "Yes. Yes, I will sign papers and allow Meghan to be adopted by Alexandra."

I could hear the sadness in her voice and I knew at that moment why both of us were crying. I whispered, "Thank you," to her. I don't know if she heard me, but I knew I was not able say anything more to her at that time.

Oliver squeezed my hand and said, "Thank you, Ellen, from both of us."

Perry continued to talk to Ellen for a short time as he explained what would need to be done from this point, but to be totally honest, I didn't hear a word. My mind was overwhelmed with so many emotions that even I was having difficulty keeping up. I did hear Perry tell her that he would call back with the time and date for her to sign and that she would not have to appear in court. And with that, the adoption proceedings were underway.

Oliver and I stood up shook hands with Perry and walked out of his office very happy people. Oliver took my hand as we walked to the car; there were just no words to be said at this time.

When I got my seat belt fastened, I looked over to Oliver who had tears rolling down his cheeks. He turned to look at me and all he kept saying was, "Thank you, Alex. Thank you so much, Alex."

As the tears began to run down my face, I leaned over and kissed my husband on the cheek and whispered, "You are very welcome, my darling. I love our daughter with all my heart, Oliver, and I promise to be the best mommy I can be to her." With that Oliver started the car and we left to go home and get Meghan.

As we were on our way home, we passed by the school that Meghan would be attending and I almost shouted for Oliver to stop the car. He slammed on the brakes so hard that we both jolted forward.

"What, Alex? What is it?" Oliver asked.

I burst out laughing at the look on his face. I couldn't help it, he looked so scared and I think I took 10 years off his life in that very moment.

He looked at me with a confused look on his face. "Alex, why are we stopping the car, and why are you laughing at me like a mad woman?" he asked.

"Oliver, we have to register Meghan for school, and we need a class list, and whatever else you have to do to put your kid in school." Oliver still had that deer in the headlights look, so I pointed to the elementary school. "We need to register Meghan for school, Oliver," I said. "I saw the flyers up around town, so while we are this close let's go see what has to be done about starting our daughter on the path to success."

With that we both laughed and Oliver pulled into the parking lot. After meeting the principal and the teachers, and getting a mountain of paper work filled out, we headed home. Oliver and I talked nonstop until we pulled into the driveway.

Meghan came running out of Mrs. Sigel's house when she saw us pull up. "Am I adopted now?" Meghan squealed as she ran and jumped into Oliver's arms.

"Not yet, baby," Oliver answered, "But it won't take long." Mrs. Sigel was standing in her doorway as we yelled thank you to her and headed inside our house.

"Meghan, we have more news for you," I said.

"What news do you have, Mommy?" Meghan asked with those big blue eyes full of wonder.

"Well, Daddy and I stopped by the school you will be going to and got you all signed up."

"Well, mostly all signed up," Oliver interjected.

I laughed, "Yeah, mostly. That sure is a lot of paperwork to fill out just to send one little girl to school."

Oliver and I looked at each other and laughed, "Guess we have a lot to learn as well Alex," Oliver said with a smile on his face.

"Hey, Meghan, do you remember Kaycee's daughter Emy?"

"Yes, I do," Meghan replied.

"Well, she will be going to the same school you will be attending, so you will already have a friend there."

"Oh, yeah, that will be fun!" Meghan yelled as she ran up the sidewalk.

Just as soon as we walked into the house, Oliver's phone rang. It was the hospital. There was a child that had been very sick for a long time, and the nurse wanted Oliver to know that little Timmy had passed away.

"I see," Oliver said softly. "Thank you for calling me." Oliver turned to me with an overwhelmingly sad look on his face and told me the sad news about Timmy.

"Oliver," I said, "I am so very sorry. He was such a sweet little boy. Now we have to trust in God that his struggles are over and he is rejoicing with our Lord right now."

Oliver smiled at me and whispered softly, "You always know what to say, Alex. Thank you." I put my arms around him and drew him to me and just held him.

As we stood there in the kitchen, Meghan came running in and suddenly stopped right in her tracks. "Why are you both so sad looking?" Meghan asked.

"Oliver turned to her and said, Meghan, there was a little boy at the hospital that was very sick for a very long time and now his suffering is over. He has gone to live with Jesus and the angels."

"So why are you sad, Daddy?" Meghan asked again with a very confused look on her face. "If he is with Jesus, shouldn't we be happy for him?"

Oliver knelt down to Meghan and put his hands on her little face. "Yes, we should little one. You are absolutely right."

With that, Meghan hugged him and told us it was time for her favorite show to come on, and then she ran to the den and turned on the television.

Oliver rose to his feet and turned to me. "I am a very blessed man, Alex. I know how much I could have lost."

I smiled softly at him and winked. "Yes, you are, Oliver." Then, with a little giggle, I walked towards my office to get some work done.

I had been in there for quite some time when Oliver entered. "Are you hungry, Alex? I thought we would go out to dinner tonight."

"That sounds like a great idea, Oliver. What are you and Meghan in the mood for?" I asked.

"Well, there is a new Italian place that just opened, and I would like to try it."

"You know, that sounds good. We haven't had Italian for quite some time, and I am sure Meghan would love it there." I smiled and got up from my desk. "Oliver, while I have been working I was also doing some thinking about things with Meghan. She is starting school and you and I are both needing to get back to our jobs. We are going to have to figure out how we are going to work this."

"You are right, Alex. We do have to go over this." Oliver walked over to me and put his arms around me. "I love you so much, Alex. I promise to make you happy for the rest of our lives.

I smiled, "I love you too, Oliver, but you are still a man, so at some point you will make me crazy and I will want to put you in time out, but I will always love you." With that, we got Meghan and left out for a nice family dinner. The new place was on the other side of town, so we listened to Meghan tell us how much she was going to do in school until we arrived. It was a nice place and we were seated very quickly. We enjoyed a wonderful meal and decided quickly this would be our new favorite Italian place. Then, we headed out the door to go home. I really was in my own little family world when my phone rang.

Chapter 22

It was Kacee calling, and when I answered she was very excited on the phone. "Hey, Alex, it's Kacee, your executive manager and best friend wondering where in the world you are? I haven't talked to you in several days, and you haven't been in the new office enough. I had to put your photo up on the wall so the new designer would know who you are," she snickered. Kacee was talking a mile a minute, which is pretty normal for her, when I finally had to interrupt.

"Kacee, I know. I am sorry, but we have so much to catch up on. I can't thank you enough for taking charge and getting us up and running. I will be in the office tomorrow morning. Please set up a staff meeting so we can all really get reacquainted, and order breakfast for everyone too, please. And Kacee, I said, I really do appreciate you. Thank you so much for being there."

"Okay, excellent. I will see you in the morning." And with that, we hung up.

Oliver was snickering. "And just what are you snickering at?" I asked him.

"Just listening to you and Kacee. I don't know how you two could ever work without the other."

I snickered too and smiled back at him. "I would be lost without her, Oliver, and it's time I showed her how much I appreciate all her efforts. You know Oliver, you need to show your appreciation for your assistant as well. She has been taking care of things while you have been out too."

"You're right. Alex, what are you doing for Kacee? I will do that too," Oliver laughed out loud and looked at me with that evil grin.

"I am going to make Kacee a full partner in the fashion house. She knows how to manage, setup, and pull off the exceptional presentations. I know how to manage the business and financials, and my personal line is doing exceptionally well. This is going to be a great fall and winter season for us. I am thankful that things are so good for us again, Oliver." I smiled and winked at him.

"Me too Alex. Me too," he whispered.

Meghan had fallen asleep in the car on the ride home, so I carried her up to her room and put her to bed. I stood there just watching her sleep, realizing yet again how very fortunate I was. There was still a little bit of regret in me that I had not given birth to her myself, but I loved her with all my heart and that is all that really mattered anyway.

Chapter 22

The next couple of weeks were so busy. Meghan had started school, the fashion house was incredibly busy, and Oliver had been honored for his dedication and love for the kids at the hospital. We were going into the holiday season, which was even busier than normal for all of us. Meghan had homework, school plays, a Christmas concert, and our church was putting on the Christmas Eve nativity scene where Meghan was one of the stars in the sky.

She was actually holding a long stick that had a star painted on it, but she took this role very seriously and we practiced several times so that she would be perfect! Our family had fallen into a well-flowing routine. I dropped Meghan off at school in the mornings at 7:15 and she got off the bus at the house of our neighbor, Mrs. Sigel, at 3:45. Oliver was there to pick her up by 4:00. It all worked, and we thrived as a family. Oliver and I prospered in our respective fields as well. I just kept thinking *how could this get any better?* Then the call came from Perry. Ellen had signed the papers and Meghan was now legally my daughter. I have to admit a part of me felt sad for Ellen, because I can imagine what it must be like to give your child away, but the bigger part of me was overjoyed at the news. I called Oliver as soon as I hung up with Perry and told him the news.

"Alexandra," Oliver started, "I love you more every day than I did the day before, and I will always know how blessed I am to have you as my wife, and the mother of my child, and, I love you."

"I love you too, Oliver!" I almost shouted the words, I was so excited. *It's all perfect, my life really is perfect* I thought to myself, and I could not erase the smile from my face all day long. Kacee came into my office and I jumped out of my chair and hugged her while telling her the news.

I think Kacee squealed louder than I did, and then we sat down and started the process of really catching up. There was so much to talk about: our families, the direction the fashion industry was going, and our dreams as moms and working women.

It was Wednesday afternoon when I called a staff meeting, and once everyone had gathered, I told them the news regarding Kacee being a full partner and how much we appreciated each and every one of them. I then told them to go home and enjoy a very Merry Christmas with their families and not to even think about work until Monday morning. Kacee handed out the Christmas bonuses and gifts from us, and everyone left except for Kacee and me.

We spent the next several hours discussing business and upcoming events. There were some events that Kaycee would handle, some that I would handle, and many that we would handle together. There were not as many out of town trips, but for the ones that would come up, we would then determine if we were going and which of us needed to go. New York was always a big deal so both of us already knew that we would always both go to fashion week there. I did surprise Kacee with the news that we had been invited to fashion week in Paris and we would both be going. We had dreamed for many years of being invited, and this week our invitation came in the mail.

I thought Kacee would jump out of her chair. "Are you serious Alex?" She squealed. "We are actually going to Paris?"

Chapter 22

I couldn't help but squeal like a school girl myself when I answered her, "YES!"

There were different levels of invites for fashion week in Paris. Everyone generally started on the viewing level, where you can look, but you can't touch, kind of thing. Next was the presentation level, where you could actually put your designs on the runway. Then came the most important level, the level where you could actually purchase someone's designs and house them in your store.

"Kacee, we have been invited to present and to purchase," I shouted. That just does not happen the first time being invited. Many times it takes years to be able to present, and some have waited decades to be able to purchase, and here we are, presenting and purchasing.

As I was telling Kacee all about this, it still seemed so unreal to me as well. "I can't believe we are going to Paris, and presenting, and purchasing!" Kacee shouted again.

"I know! This is crazy!" I said as I leaned forward and hugged Kacee with all I had in me. "Thank you, Kacee! Thank you for sticking with me over the years. We are there!"

"I never thought we wouldn't be, Alex." Kacee had tears in her eyes as I opened the bottle of champagne and we toasted ourselves. I sat there silently for a few minutes, and Kacee looked at me and said, "I have nothing to wear to Paris!"

I can't remember laughing that hard in a long time, as we looked around at our amazing designs that were hanging all over the place. We looked at each other and at the same time said, "We will find something!" What a great day; what a great time; what a great adventure unfolding in front of us.

After a few more hours of work and catching up, we finally called it a day, wished each other a very Merry Christmas and left for our homes. As I sat in my car driving home, I realized how much had happened in the last couple of years. I was a mother, a business owner, and still sane (well somewhat sane) I snickered to myself. I exhaled and said out loud, "I am okay!" I couldn't help but feel such a sense of fulfillment and accomplishment. More than all of that, I felt blessed by God. He gave me all of this, he led me down my path and I know that I couldn't have survived without him in my life. I pulled in the driveway, bowed my head, and thanked God for the blessings.

Chapter 23

The holidays flew by and Meghan, Oliver, and I enjoyed the best Christmas ever. We spent time with family and friends and relished in the love of the season. We knew it was time to take Meghan up to the family cabin and meet our friend Colt, if he were around somewhere. I had read in the Times of the success of a restaurant that had been opened a few years ago. The food, the service, and the atmosphere, made this the place to be in NYC, and our friend Colt just happened to be the owner. I smiled thinking of him and how this unexpected friend had played such a big part in our lives when our lives were falling apart.

I told Oliver I was going to give Colt a call and see how he was.

Oliver looked at me and smiled and said, "I was just thinking about him the other day. Yes, Alex, give him a call." I dialed his number and to my surprise he answered.

"Alex!" he said with excitement, "How are ya girl?"

I laughed and answered him, "I am good Colt. We are all good. Merry Christmas, and Happy New Year!" I said.

"Same to you all too," he said. We talked on the phone for almost an hour and then he shared some very heartwarming news. "Alex, I have met someone, and she is a very nice lady. I have spent some time with her and even invited her to the farm a couple of times. She enjoys riding horses..."

"So you put her on Ms. Lacy?" I interrupted.

Colt laughed. "No, Ms. Lacy is for the not-so-experienced riders I have met over the years."

"Hey, wait," I laughed, and Colt laughed with me.

"I really like her, Alex," he said softly. "I don't have any plans as yet, but I do know I enjoy her company, and I think Cassie would understand, don't you?" he asked.

"Yes Colt," I said, "Cassie would under-stand, as long as you don't paint the barn any other color but pink." We both laughed and he assured me that would never happen, and with that we exchanged our goodbyes and hung up the phone.

I went and sat down by Oliver and told him, "Colt has a lady friend, and he sounds like he is great!"

Meghan was ready for bed and it was time for all of us to call it a night. Oliver and I tucked Meghan into bed, and Oliver read her a story as I sat and held her little hand. *She is growing up so quickly,* I thought as I looked at her sleepy eyes. Oliver and I cherished these moments, both of us knowing that they were passing so fast.

Once Meghan was fast asleep, Oliver and I quietly slipped out her door and walked hand in hand to our bedroom. I just kept thinking to myself, *this can't get much better than this.* I felt a warm and complete feeling as I climbed into bed and cuddled up to the man I would love forever. "I love you Oliver," I whispered.

"I love you too Alex," he answered, and with that we both fell asleep.

Chapter 24

I was up early the next day, knowing I had to get Meghan ready for school and get to the fashion house. There was so much to do before Kacee and I left for Paris. I couldn't be any more excited, and the thought of the long work hours ahead of us didn't bother me in the least.

I dropped Meghan off and was headed for the office when Kacee called. "Hey, Alex, are you on your way?" she asked.

"Yes, I am about 3 blocks away. What kind of donuts do you want, Kacee?" I laughed.

She laughed on the phone and said, "Oh Alex, you know me too well..." Then the pause, and we both said, "Chocolate filled," at the same time.

I laughed as I pulled into the Dunkin Donuts. I walked in the door and the young girl behind the counter smiled and asked if I wanted the usual. I nodded my head yes, and couldn't help but laugh out loud. She smiled and asked me, "Why are you laughing?" Both of us knowing the answer. "It's Monday," we both said together. She boxed up the goodies and coffee, and I was on my way.

It was a great work week, and the next couple of weeks were just as great. The line was finished and we were ready for Paris. Kacee had booked our hotel, our flight, and even the first night's dinner reservations. We would be leaving for Paris in the morning, and there was still so much to do at work and at home.

I was sad about leaving Meghan and Oliver behind, but a part of me was like a school girl who had just been asked to the prom. Except I already had the dress!

I don't think I had slept a wink when the alarm clock went off. I am pretty sure my feet didn't even touch the floor as I was hurrying Meghan down the stairs and to the breakfast table. She finished her oatmeal and I had my coffee ready in hand as I all but pushed us both out the door. I was so excited I forgot to tell Oliver goodbye.

He came running out to the car and gave me a kiss goodbye. "Call me when you land," he smiled, and with that I pulled from the driveway to take Meghan to school.

I reminded her on the way to the school drop off line that Daddy would be picking her up and taking her to school for the next week. She was excited that Daddy would be taking her to school because he let her eat in the car, and Mommy wouldn't. I told her how much I loved her and kissed her goodbye as she got out of the car and ran to meet her friends. She was growing and changing every day, and as a Mom, I was excited and sad at the same time. I smiled and waved to her on my way by.

The drive to the office seemed like it took forever. I wanted to get this adventure started. "Paris! I am going to Paris," I said out loud. I was almost giddy when I pulled into the fashion house. Kacee was everywhere, doing this and that, getting everything just so and explaining all the ins and outs to the office manager. I couldn't help but laugh as I pulled Kacee out the door.

"Come on Kacee!" You are driving her crazy. Let's go!" I shouted. Kacee was still giving instructions as I pulled her out the door. We are going to miss our flight if you don't stop barking orders,

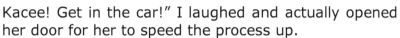

Kacee! Get in the car!" I laughed and actually opened her door for her to speed the process up.

We were at the airport in no time, and it was hard to keep our excitement controlled as we went through security. The security guard looked at us like we were crazy, as we giggled like a couple of junior high girls. We breezed through the check points and practically ran to find our terminal.

I was trying to keep up with Kacee, who was now several steps ahead of me, when she stopped dead in her tracks, turned to me and said in a high-pitched voice, "We have arrived."

I couldn't help but laugh at Kacee as I began to search my purse for my ticket. I was getting a little frantic due to the fact that I couldn't put my hands on it when Kacee busted out laughing. I looked up to see her holding my ticket in her hand doing that Nanny Nanny Boo Boo little dance thing like she was in second grade.

I grabbed my ticket out of her hand and went up to the attendant who, like the security guard, looked at us like we had just lost our minds. I explained to her we were going to Paris, and she looked at me without sharing my excitement and said, "Yes ma'am, you are." It dawned on me that she would probably already know that since she worked there but to be honest I didn't really care. We were heading to Paris for our first invited fashion show and I didn't care who knew how excited we were.

We boarded the plane and, to my surprise, Kacee had booked us in first class. I had never flown first class. It never really mattered to me. So long as the plane didn't crash, I was happy to be seated wherever. Kacee and I took our seats and settled in for the long flight. We both said we would nap on the way but we both also knew there was no way that was going to happen.

It didn't take long until Kacee and I were deep in business conversation. When the flight attendant brought us warm towels and champagne, I looked at Kacee and thanked her for taking care of the travel arrangements. I never had to worry about any of this part because she had it handled every time.

We went over our fashion line that we would be presenting, and Kacee was on the phone finishing up the details regarding the day models we had hired. Although our fashion house was doing well with our designs and our purchasing, I was still not comfortable with retaining full-time models as many of the larger fashion houses did. We had always gone through the temp services and had never had a problem.

The time flew by so quickly, and in no time the pilot came over the intercom telling us that we would be landing soon. We had everything finalized when we hit the tarmac. Kacee had arranged for a car to be there waiting for us, so we did not have to try to hail a cab, or whatever they are called, in Paris. Our driver was standing there holding a sign with the fashion house's name on it. I have to admit, for an instant I felt like someone very important.

Kacee must have known exactly what I was thinking, because she looked at me and said, "Yes, we are that important." We both laughed and headed to baggage claim. Our clothing line had already been shipped over and our liaison had arranged fittings with the models, so all we needed at this point was to find our hotel, freshen up, and find some dinner.

Kacee and I were in awe of the beauty of Paris from our first step off the plane. There was so much to see, and I was looking forward to taking as much of it in as time allowed. Our driver had us at our hotel in no time and we were quickly checked in and taken to our suite.

The view was breathtaking, and the opulence of our room was something I would imagine royalty were accustomed to. We, on the other hand, were not, and Kacee and I both knew we were going to enjoy this adventure.

The restaurant where Kacee had made our reservations was within walking distance from our hotel, so we decided to walk. On our way out, the concierge asked if we needed anything or if we needed a car. We thanked him and said no. We wanted to enjoy the warm evening and take in the surroundings. The concierge was a little skeptical of our plans to walk and asked again if he could get a car for us. I smiled and thanked him again, and with that we strolled out the door.

I think we stopped at every window to take in all this street had to offer. There was just so much activity around us, it was a little intimidating. I then understood why the concierge was somewhat insistent regarding getting us a car, but we arrived at the restaurant without any issues.

We enjoyed a wonderful bottle of wine, and our dinner was exceptional. We even followed up with dessert. The pace of the dinner hour was much slower here. No one seemed to be in a rush to eat and move on to their next destination.

In the fashion industry, you spend a lot of time people watching and doing personal clothing assessments on strangers. I always try to be kind in my views, but sometimes I just have to wonder...*what were you thinking putting that outfit together?*

Kacee and I were almost 2 hours into dinner when my phone rang and it was Oliver and Meghan.

Meghan had to talk first. "Mommy, how was your airplane ride? What does Paris look like? What time are you coming home? I need you to read a story to me tonight before I get too sleepy to listen." Meghan asked so many questions I had to interrupt her just to get a word in.

"I had a great flight. Paris is beautiful! Daddy will have to read you a story tonight. Mommy will be home in a few days" I said to her with sadness in my voice. "Meghan?" I asked, "Where is Daddy?"

"He is right here. I gotta go do my homework now. Love you Mom!" Meghan shouted.

"I love you too baby," I said, but I knew at that point she was gone and Oliver was now on the phone.

"Hey honey," Oliver said. "Sounds like all went well with the flight. Are you settled in?" Oliver asked.

"Yes, the flight was great and the hotel is amazing. We are actually finishing up dinner right now. Oliver, we have to come back here for a family vacation, even if we just come to this restaurant," I laughed.

"That good huh?" Oliver laughed.

As Oliver and I were having our conversation, Kacee's phone rang and it was Emy calling her. I could hear Emy asking a million questions, like Meghan had, and Kacee answered and asked where Emy's daddy was. I couldn't help but laugh at Kacee, and Oliver asked me what I was laughing at.

"Oh, nothing dear. Just happy to hear your voice, and Meghan's as well," I answered. Oliver and I finished our conversation about the time Kacee and her husband did, so we said our goodbyes and hung up our phones.

Kacee asked me if I was finished and if I wanted to go back to the hotel or get a car and see Paris at night. I laughed at her and said, "We have to go to the hotel now. The show starts tomorrow, and I want to get

a good night's sleep." We both laughed out loud, both of us knowing neither of us would sleep tonight.

We walked slowly back to our hotel, enjoying the stars in the sky and discussing the activities that were to come tomorrow. The concierge greeted us at the inner hotel doors and asked how dinner was.

"It was amazing!" Kacee said, and I nodded my head in agreement.

"That's splendid," he said. "Now would either of you ladies care for any kind of evening refreshment to be sent up to your suite, or can I get a table for you in our piano lounge?"

"Oh, no, thank you," I said, "We are calling it a night. We have a very big day tomorrow, but maybe tomorrow evening we will," I said with a warm smile on my face.

"Very well ladies. Will you be requiring a wake-up call for the morning?"

"Oh, that might be very helpful. I doubt if we will get any sleep, but just in case, will you ring our suite at 6:30?" I asked.

"Yes, of course," he said, and wished us a good night.

Chapter 25

Once we went to our suite, Kacee settled into her pajamas and was attempting to work the remote while I headed for a hot bath. It had been a long day, and I knew I was ready to relax and enjoy some bubble time. The bath was extremely relaxing and I almost fell asleep in the tub, so I decided that before I drowned I should get out and go to bed.

I got dressed for bed as quietly as possible, since I wasn't sure if Kacee had gone to bed and did not want to wake her. I opened the bathroom door to find Kacee sound asleep on the couch with the remote still in her hand, but the television wasn't on. I couldn't help but giggle, wondering if she ever got it to work or just fell asleep trying. I decided not to wake her, so I covered her up, grabbed my laptop and went into my room.

I was thinking that I needed to look over some last minute things regarding the next day, but my eyelids took charge and I don't believe I turned over until I heard the courtesy call from the front desk waking us up. I slowly moved towards the kitchen to make us some coffee, only to find Kacee sitting at the table, dressed and ready to go with a cup of coffee already in her hand. I looked at her with wonder and a slight smile came across her face.

"Yes Alex, I am up and ready," Kacee laughed. "I am just waiting for you to get motivated, so let's go already!"

"Kacee," I said, "You are too much, just too much," as I stumbled to the coffee maker. I fixed my coffee and headed to my room to dress and put on makeup. This was going to be the start of several very

♥♥♥♥♥♥♥♥♥♥♥♥♥♥

long days, but several very exciting days. We had so much to do today even before the show started that I was beginning to feel the excitement building up in me as well.

"Okay, I am ready now," I said as I looked at myself in the mirror. I was nervous and excited and ready, just so very ready, to go. I walked into the living area to find that Kacee had changed clothes from the outfit I had just seen her in. "A little nervous are we," I said, as I looked her up and down and laughed.

"Oh hush," she said, "Let's go. I have a car waiting for us." We got down to the front desk where a different concierge greeted us and asked if we needed anything. "No," Kacee said with a huge smile on her face, "We are good."

We went out to find a limo waiting for us. I looked at Kacee with a wondering look on my face, "A limo?" I asked.

Kacee looked at me with the same wondering look on her face. "I didn't call for a limo," she whispered to me, "I just called for a town car for us."

We both stood there as the driver tipped his hat and opened the door for us. I looked at him and before I could ask, he smiled and said, "Compliments of the event hosts."

"Oh how awesome is this!" Kacee squealed as she all but leapt into the car. "Oh, Alex, there are mimosa's in here waiting for us! Get in!" she shouted.

Our driver couldn't help but chuckle. As I walked by, I whispered to him, "She doesn't get out much." With that he laughed out loud and closed the door behind me.

Kacee was handing me my glass before I had even sat all the way down. "Thank you," I smiled to

♥ ♥ ♥ ♥ ♥ ♥ ♥ ♥ ♥ ♥ ♥ ♥ ♥

her and said with a laugh, "I knew I needed some orange juice today." We smiled and toasted each other and sipped on our beverages as our driver began giving us the tour of Paris.

He pointed out some of the most amazing things and said, "I am at your disposal for the next 2 days. By the way, my name is Anthony." I guess the look on our faces was amusing to him as he chuckled a bit.

"Well, Anthony, it is very nice to meet you. Thank you for taking care of us for the next couple of days," I said softly. He tipped his hat again and took us to the venue.

"Ladies," Anthony said, "The show begins promptly at 10:00, and the hosts will be there to greet you, so I will be delivering you to the back entrance where all of your models should be already be in hair and makeup. Here is a map of the venue, and if you should have any questions, your personal concierge will be happy to help."

"Thank you, Anthony," I said as we were pulling up to the back entrance.

Anthony quickly jumped out and opened our door for us. "My pleasure, ladies. Good luck today," he said and once again tipped his hat to us.

Chapter 26

Kacee looked at me wide-eyed and said, "This place is huge, Alex. We'd better get going so we can find our area and meet our models."

I shook my head in agreement as we walked through the doorway to what would be the biggest day of our careers.

We must have looked a bit lost, as a very handsome young man walked up to us and said, "You must be Alex and Kacee from Excellence Fashion House and Design."

We both smiled and said, "Yes, we are."

"Well, it's a pleasure to meet you. I am Stephon and I will be your concierge while you are here. Please follow me."

Stephon lead us down a long corridor to the greeting room where we met the hosts, who welcomed us like we were the ones to be in awe of. Kacee and I stood there enjoying the company of some of the greatest fashion designers in the world, and soon we were being escorted to where our models were. Kacee had arranged for eight models so they would only be changing four times, thus cutting down on cost and garment confusion. Even though this was our first time here in Paris, this was not our first fashion show, and over the years we had learned the ins and outs of this business. Too many models created unnecessary confusion, which could lead to a design not being matched up with the right accessories, which could cost us thousands of dollars.

Kacee and I met our models and thanked them for wearing our designs. Kacee stood watch over the hair and makeup, as we had already determined what hair and makeup went with each outfit.

Stephon came to gather Kacee and me to escort us to our seats as the show was about to begin. Our seats were exceptional. It was our first time invited and our seats were second row. That is a big deal. Anyone who knows how the seating is arranged knows the value of getting in the first, second, or third row. Anything beyond the third row is just filler! We sat there taking notes on designs as they came down the runway and anxiously awaited the arrival of our designs.

Paris was somewhat different than the other shows we had been to. Normally either Kacee or I would be behind the stage with our models awaiting our turn to display our designs. However, in Paris your concierge took control of all of the behind the scenes, so the designer, buyer, or company representative was able to watch the other designers' work. I had mixed feelings about this because I didn't want to miss a thing, but I also did not trust anyone else to run the show the same way Kacee or I would.

Although Excellence had been in business for many years, producing our own line was relatively new territory for us, but I guess we would do what our hosts expected of us.

As I sat there working all of this out in my mind, I did not notice Stephon standing there beside me. "Excuse me, Ms. Alex," Stephon softly whispered, "but would you come with me, please?"

Kacee looked at me and had begun to gather our stuff, when I said softly to her, "Please stay here. I can handle whatever this is, but we need you to continue taking notes and pictures. I will be back in no

time." I said, trying to convince Kacee as well as myself.

Stephon briskly walked me backstage to the waiting area that was designated for our models. I quickly counted seven models. I looked at Stephon, and before he could speak I said, "There are seven models, but we are to have eight. Is someone in the bathroom?" I asked.

"No, Ms. Alex," Stephon said. "One of your models has fallen ill and has been taken to the hospital."

"Taken to the hospital?" I asked. "I just saw all eight of them thirty minutes ago and they were fine. What happened?" I asked.

"I am not sure," Stephon answered. I guess the look I shot at him must have been one of annoyance, because he stepped back from me and asked what I would like to do regarding the change in our production.

I looked at him and asked, "Where are the designs she was to wear?"

"Your designs are in your staff room," he answered.

I looked at the clock, and then to him. "How much time do we have?"

Stephon said, "You will be presenting in 12 minutes."

"Okay, I will be right back," and with that I all but ran to our staff room. I found the outfits that were to be worn, held them up to me, and decided that the show must go on. I dressed myself, clipped my hair up and put on those 6-inch heels. I looked in the mirror and thought, *what are the odds the shoes would fit?* I couldn't help but laugh, thinking, *this is crazy! I have never modeled in my life.* As those thoughts were running through my head, I ran to the staging area where my models were lined up.

Stephon looked at me and smiled a huge smile. "You really are cool under pressure, aren't you?"

"I always try to look that way," I said with a little fear in my voice.

Then Stephon, in an authoritative voice, stepped to the curtain and introduced Excellence Fashion House and Designs from the United States. Our first model stepped out onto the runway with the rest of us in tow. The pace was very fast, and I don't think I took a breath the entire time. I did find Kacee in the crowd and the look on her face almost made me burst out laughing. I then realized I would not be able to look at her for the remaining time that we were showing our line. I held my head up high and walked just as fast and purposeful as the other models, and without breaking my neck, I made it through the first viewing.

The change time we were allowed was approximately 15 minutes. It was barely enough time to get to our room, change, and be lined up when once again Stephon announced we were Excellence Fashion House and Design of the United States, and we went out again. The catwalk seemed shorter the second time and we were back to the changing room once again. Then the third line was shown, and we were now in line waiting for the fourth and final line from our company to be presented. Stephon took my hand and led me to the back of the line. I almost felt like I was in trouble and the look on my face must have told him that.

"No, Ms. Alex, you are fine," he said softly. "I just need to make this correction in the line presentation."

Chapter 26

♥ ♥ ♥ ♥ ♥ ♥ ♥ ♥ ♥ ♥ ♥ ♥

"Okay, Stephon. I am trusting in your experience to know what you are doing."

Stephon smiled and then took the stage to announce us for the fourth and final time. I walked down the runway, and I did look at Kacee this time. She smiled the biggest smile and mouthed the word, "Excellence!"

As I was about to reach the curtain to go backstage, Stephon stopped me and turned me around to face the audience. "With great pleasure, I present Ms. Alex to you," Stephon said to the crowd. "Ms. Alex is the owner of Excellence Fashion House and Design, and on her first invitation to our show she had to step into her own designs and accessories as one of her models fell ill. This, ladies and gentlemen, is what makes our industry great. Ms. Alex, we welcome you and Excellence Fashion House and Design to Paris."

The roar of applause was almost deafening. I waved to the audience and mouthed, "Thank you," then turned and continued to backstage like I had done this a million times.

I looked at Stephon with a quizzical look and then embraced him, like I had known him all my life. "Thank you, Stephon, but why did you introduce me like that?" I asked.

Stephon stood back and held my hands. "Ms. Alex, I am not just your concierge. My father is Jacquez, of Jacquez Defined Fashions, and he has been watching you for years. It was my honor to be here to meet you and to help propel you and your fashion house to superstardom. You see Alexis, my father watched your business savviness as a buyer and told me then that you would be a force when you finally decided to create your own line.

"I don't even know what to say, Stephon, and that doesn't happen too often, I have to admit." We both laughed and then I felt a tap on my shoulder.

I turned around to find Jacquez standing there behind me. "Hello, Ms. Alex. It is nice to finally meet you in person. I have admired your business sense for many years, and now being here to watch you unveil your line on stage in Paris is quite an honor for me."

I was so shocked that when I finally did form words, I thanked him for the very kind words and told him I had known of his work ever since I knew that I wanted to go into the fashion industry.

"I am humbled by your kind words," Jacquez said, "And I look forward to dinner with you and Ms. Kacee at my home tonight."

"Dinner at your home tonight?" I asked.

"Of course. Didn't Stephon tell you? We would love to have you as our guests this evening. Dinner will be at 8:00, and Anthony will pick you up at, say, 6:30, if that works for you?" Jacquez asked.

Oh YES! I wanted to scream, but softly I said softly, "6:30 will be perfect. We very much look forward to this evening."

Jacquez reached out, took my hand, and kissed it. "Then tonight," he said, and turned and walked away.

I looked at Stephon like I was dreaming all of this, but when I heard Kacee's voice it was like, *Okay, now I know I am awake.*

Chapter 27

I turned and there she was all but running up the hallway to me. "Alex, what happened to our model? Why didn't you come back and get me? You were great by the way. Were you just talking to THE Jacquez? Why didn't you change heels for the third line? When did you take modeling classes? How did you learn to walk that way? And..."

"Wait Kacee," I laughed and held my hand up. "One question or statement at a time. First, our model got sick and was taken to the hospital. We need to send her flowers. Second, I have never taken modeling classes and I just walked the same way the other models walked. But I have to be honest, Kacee, they walk incredibly fast." I laughed. "Yes, I was talking to The Jacquez and we have been invited to his home for dinner tonight. Anthony will be picking us up a 6:30, and dinner is at 8. Oh, and about those shoes, I like them. That's why I didn't change."

Kacee stood there staring at me with a—my-brain-is-trying-to-process-all-of-this, look. I laughed out loud, thinking that this must have been the way I was looking at Stephon while he was answering all of my questions. The show was over and it was a huge success. All of today's designs were amazing, and I was especially proud of ours. We had worked very hard to get to this point and we measured up to the other designers.

Kacee and I finished gathering and packing up our fashions. They would now be shipped back to the States; back to our factory where we would supply the upcoming orders.

We walked outside to find Anthony waiting for us. He opened our door and we slid into the limo where hot tea and pastries were waiting for us. "Oh, Anthony," I said, "This is amazing! Thank you so much.

"You are very welcome, ladies," he said with a smile. "How did it go?" Anthony asked. Before I could even open my mouth Kacee was filling him full of the day's events. It was humorous to listen and watch her as she described how everything unfolded today. In no time at all we were back at the hotel.

Anthony jumped out of the limo, opened our door and helped us out of the limo. He tipped his hat and told us he would be back at 6:30 to collect us for dinner."

"Thank you, Anthony," both Kacee and I said at the same time, and we walked into the hotel. The concierge greeted us as we walked in and asked if there was anything that we needed. I did say yes this time, as we needed flowers sent to the hospital to our model who had gotten ill.

I looked at him and said, "I am so embarrassed. I don't remember her name or even what hospital she was taken to."

"Not to worry Ms. Alex. I will take care of all of that for you," he said.

I thanked him, and as Kacee and I were walking towards the elevator I looked at her and said, "We haven't seen that concierge before. How did he know my name?"

She looked at me, shrugged her shoulders, and said, "I don't know."

It was about 4:30 when we got to our suite, so that did not allow us a lot of time before we were to be picked up for dinner. I told Kacee I was going to jump

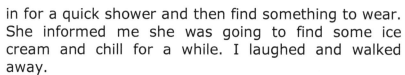

in for a quick shower and then find something to wear. She informed me she was going to find some ice cream and chill for a while. I laughed and walked away.

Just as I was about to step in the shower, Kacee yelled, "Alex, you have got to get in here!"

I grabbed a towel, wrapped myself up and hurried into the living room. "What? Kacee, I was just about to ..."

"Shut up!" she said. "Shut up and look at the television screen!"

I turned to look at the screen to find that my appearance on the runway had been televised. I slowly sat down on the couch and told Kacee to turn the TV up. The fashion journalist was talking about Excellence Fashion House from America, and how the owner, Alex Ash, had stepped in for one of the models who had fallen ill. It also showed where Stephon had announced me to the audience and the standing ovation I had received.

I sat there silently for a while until Kacee startled me back to reality with her squeal. "Alex that is how the concierge knew who you were. You are famous."

I told her I was not famous, and then smiled and said, "...yet." Kacee and I both knew what this meant; we were about to move straight to the top of the fashion world. "Kacee, I couldn't do this without you, and I will tell everyone who will listen that it's not just me here."

Kacee looked at me and smiled, "I know Alex, but I am not the spotlight kind of person. You fit that bill, and besides, one of us has to be the one to drive the getaway car." I looked at her with a bit of confusion, and she said, "You know, when the paparazzi won't leave you alone." We both laughed and I had begun to walk towards the shower when Kacee called my name. "Alex," she said, "You are going to be the face of Excellence Fashion House and Design, and I thank you for taking me along on this journey with you."

I smiled and said, "Kacee, the fun is just beginning," and at the same time with both said, "And the work!" Both of us laughed and I continued to the shower.

I stood in the shower letting the hot water cascade over me, losing track of my thoughts and the time. Kacee startled me by knocking on the door. "Alex, how long are you going to be in there? It's almost time for Anthony to pick us up."

I shouted over the shower, "On my way out now!" I didn't realize how long I had been in the shower and when I looked at the clock and it was 6:10, "Oh, crap!" I shouted. I could hear Kacee laughing at me from the other room. "I can hear you, ya know!"

She laughed louder and said, "I know!"

I walked out of my room, dressed and ready to go with three minutes to spare. *Pretty good job,* I thought to myself. Kacee and I caught the elevator and as we stepped off, there stood Anthony waiting for us at the hotel entrance.

He smiled and tipped his hat. "Good evening, ladies. You both look beautiful tonight."

Kacee and I both smiled at him and, together, said, "Thank you." Anthony closed the door behind us as we got into the limo.

Kacee looked at me and said softly, "I could really get used to this, Alex."

I looked at her and smiled, "Yeah, me too."

Chapter 27

♥♥♥♥♥♥♥♥♥♥♥♥♥

"Ladies," Anthony said, "There is chilled champagne to your right, and light hors d'oeuvres to your left. Please help yourselves to whatever you would like. Kacee and I both decided to skip the champagne, but I could not restrain myself from the amazing looking petit fours that were laid out so perfectly.

I looked at Kacee and laughed. "If we keep eating like this, we will be hitting the treadmill harder than we already do."

Kacee looked at me and laughed, and then just like a light had gone off in her head, she said, "We need a workout room at the fashion house, Alex. That would be a great stress reliever and then we could eat like this all the time."

I kind of thought she was joking at first, but as I watched the wheels turning in her head I knew it was just a matter of time before this idea came to fruition. I shook my head and smiled at Kacee and thought, *you really do come up with some great ideas most of the time.* I looked at her and said, "Yeah, you just want more ice cream at work don't ya?" We both laughed and said yes at the same time. We had turned to look out our windows at the breathtaking view of the countryside when Anthony announced we were almost at Jacquez's home.

Kacee and I immediately started touching up our makeup and hair, both of us asking the other the same question, "Do I look okay?" We both laughed as Anthony did too, and he assured us we both looked quite lovely. As we pulled up to the front entrance I was very impressed immediately with the manicured grounds and the never-ending house we were about to enter.

Jacquez greeted us outside and introduced us to his strikingly beautiful wife, Camarra. Kacee and I both extended our hands but were quickly greeted with hugs from this lovely lady.

"Please, ladies," Camarra said and motioned for us to follow her, "Let's go inside and find something to eat. I am starving!"

Jacquez looked at her and said, "My darling, you are always starving, and yet you look like a never-ending beauty at all times." Kacee and I turned to each other and mouthed aww...and with that we went inside. The foyer was larger than my entire house, I thought to myself, yet I was more impressed with Camarra's welcoming and warm personality than any of their more than lavish possessions. We walked into a grand living room where everything looked meticulously polished and placed, and yet again I felt very at home there. Jacquez invited us to sit down and without hesitation he began to talk business.

"There is greatness I see in you and your fashion house, Alex, and I want to see you succeed in this very competitive industry," Jacquez said to me.

"I am flattered that you have spent time researching our company and our designs. I look forward to knowing your experience in the field of design lines. I have for many years purchased other designers' clothing lines, and when the opportunity came for us to design and present our own line, I can't tell you how nervous we really were," I said.

Kacee looked at me and shook her head. "Yes, we were nervous to present our first line, but all of us have the utmost confidence in Alex. We were confident that she would lead us into this new adventure, and that it would be successful."

♥ ♥ ♥ ♥ ♥ ♥ ♥ ♥ ♥ ♥ ♥ ♥ ♥

Camarra looked at Kacee and said, "Kacee, it is obvious you have great respect for Alex and what you all do, and that, my dear, is a wonderful thing to see."

Kacee smiled at Camarra and said softly, "Thank you. You are right, I do."

Camarra then stood up and told us it was time for dinner, and she was starving. We all laughed and followed her into their kitchen. I guess I assumed we would be dining in the formal dining area, and I think I assumed other people would be joining us, but I was incorrect. The kitchen was warm and inviting, and very, very large, but still inviting. We all sat down at the island in the center of the kitchen where the meal that was cooking smelled heavenly. I guess I assumed once again that this had been prepared by a chef, or even catered, until I saw Camarra wrap her apron around her waist and begin to stir whatever was simmering in front of us.

Camarra looked at me and said, "Do you enjoy cooking, Alex?" I nodded my head yes, as I was enjoying the wine that Jacquez had poured for us.

I smiled and said to her, "I enjoy cooking. I am just not very good at it for the most part."

Kacee looked at me and laughed out loud, then looked at Camarra and said, "Ask her about the turkey she fixed for Christmas."

Camarra giggled at Kacee and said to me, "Okay Alex, tell me about your Christmas turkey."

I looked at Kacee with an oh, no you didn't, look, and said, "I would prefer not to if you don't mind."

Everyone laughed and Jacquez lifted his glass. "I would like to propose a toast. To new friends, new adventures, great success, and my lovely wife's wonderful cooking!" We all lifted our glasses and began to enjoy this meal that Camarra had made by hand, that was so good it should have been served in a restaurant.

The evening flew by, and we had enjoyed several hours with Jacquez and Camarra when I realized it was 2 am and we had to be back at the showing by 9. I looked at Jacquez and said, "It's 2 am, and we really need to let you good people get some sleep. I am sorry we stayed so long, but I have to be honest, I have enjoyed every minute of it."

Kacee rose to her feet and shook her head in agreement with me, then said, "Thank you both for inviting us into your beautiful home and for the delicious dinner. Reluctantly I have to agree with Alex," she said, "We really do need to get going so we will be ready for tomorrow."

Camarra looked at Jacquez in confusion. "Didn't you invite them to stay the night here?" she asked. "I sent Anthony home hours ago,"

Jacquez looked at us and said, "Well, ladies, will you be staying as our guests tonight?"

"Oh, that is so incredibly kind and generous of you both, but we really couldn't impose on you like that," I said. "Also, we didn't bring anything with us. All of our stuff is back at the hotel."

Jacquez looked at us and smiled, "You may not have heard of me, but I am a fashion designer, and I am sure somewhere in this house we can find something for you two to sleep in and something to wear back to your hotel in the morning."

"It's already morning," Camarra snickered, "So you all need to get some sleep before you head off to the show. You wouldn't want to miss day two of fashion week ya know."

Chapter 27

♥ ♥ ♥ ♥ ♥ ♥ ♥ ♥ ♥ ♥ ♥ ♥ ♥

I looked at her with a quizzical look on my face and asked, "Won't you be coming with Jacquez to the show?"

"Oh, no dear," she said. "I have been to many, many of these shows all over the world and I am quite content to see the highlights on the television and listen to Jacquez's stories when he comes home.

"Ladies," Camarra said, "If you will follow me, I will show you to your rooms." Kacee almost jumped when Camarra told us to follow her. I couldn't help but laugh to myself at her excitement.

We walked up the stairs and down an incredibly long hallway to our rooms. Upon opening the door to my room, I realized that this room was larger than the suite we were staying in at the hotel. It was breathtaking, and the bed was truly the largest bed I had ever seen in my life. I found pajamas laid out for me on the bed, and I have to admit I almost felt like a little girl, I wanted to jump on that bed so badly. I had to laugh out loud. *No, Alex,* I said to myself, *you are not going to jump on the bed like Meghan does. You are going to go wash your face and get some sleep! Okay!* I said to myself as though I was in trouble.

I washed up and dressed for bed and was just about to turn down the covers when there was knock at my door and Kacee stood there in her pajamas that matched mine. I looked at her and we both busted out laughing. Kacee ran and actually jumped in the middle of my bed.

"Alex", she laughed, "Have you ever seen a bed this big in your life?"

"No," I laughed, "And those were my exact same words! Kacee, this has been the most amazing adventure so far, and we haven't even made it to day 2 of the show!"

"I know, Alex. Today has been an incredibly long day, but I have had more excitement today than I have had in years, and I have Emy!"

"I totally understand, Kacee. This has been amazing!"

It was 7:15 when I was awakened by the soft music that was being piped into my room. *What a great way to wake up in the morning!* I thought. Kacee had fallen asleep in my room and soon awoke to the music playing as well.

"Good morning, Alex," she whispered. "What time is it?"

"It is 7:20, and we need to get a move on if we are going to make it to the hotel, shower, dress, and get to the show by 9."

Kacee sprang to her feet and all but ran towards the door, flinging it open like it was made of air. In her haste, she almost tripped over a box that had been left outside my door. She laughed, picked up the box, and brought it to me. She then went to her door and found a box waiting there as well. Sometime in the night, someone had brought us clothing to wear back to our hotel.

"These are original Jacquez designs we are going to wear!" Kacee whispered with so much excitement in her voice she squealed. I didn't even have words, I just opened my box and turned to show Kacee what I would be wearing, but she had already gone to her room to get dressed.

We walked out of our rooms at the same time, and the dresses we were wearing were absolute perfection. "You look great, Kacee," I said.

"You do too, Alex," she said and grinned. We walked downstairs to find Camarra serving breakfast in the kitchen.

"Excellent timing, ladies. Breakfast is ready, and you both look amazing this morning."

"Thank you Camarra," I said.

"You are most welcome. Now, ladies," Camarra said, "Grab yourselves a plate and let's have some breakfast."

"Oh, we really can't stay. We have so much to do today. Your hospitality has been more than generous towards us. Everything looks and smells divine." I said.

"Oh, poppycock, Alex. You need to have a good breakfast to get you through your long day. Didn't your mother tell you that every day of your growing years?" Camarra said and smiled.

"Yes, ma'am, she did," and before I could say another word Camarra presented me with a plate that would feed three starving people.

"There is a lot I have learned over the years, ladies," Camarra stated as she raised her coffee cup, "And one of the most important lessons in life that I subscribe to is to start each day fresh and value what you can do for yourself and others. And besides, I was starving, so I had to fix enough to hold me over for the day, or at least until lunch, but that's our little secret." Camarra winked at us and we all enjoyed our breakfast.

Soon Anthony was standing in the door way. "Good morning, Anthony. Come and enjoy some breakfast with us," Camarra said as she smiled and got up from her chair.

"Oh, no, thank you, Ms. Camarra," Anthony smiled and said. "It was grandparent's morning at school, so I had breakfast with my granddaughter."

"Oh, how lovely. I am sure Sasha loved having her papa there with her. When are you bringing her by to see us again?" Camarra asked.

"I will bring her by soon, Ms. Camarra. She loves coming to see you and Jacquez, and she especially loves tending to your flower garden with you," Anthony said and smiled. He then looked at Kacee and me and motioned with his hand, "Ladies, are we ready to go?"

Kacee and I stood up and thanked Camarra for her gracious hospitality and delicious breakfast. "Ladies, please come visit us again soon, and you are more than welcome to stay with us any time."

"Thank you, Camarra. That is so very kind of you," I said, and Anthony led us to the waiting car.

I looked at Kacee once we had gotten in the limo and asked, "Have you ever felt so welcomed anywhere in your life as we did at the home of THE Jacquez?"

Kacee lifted her mimosa to me and smiled. "No I haven't, and yes I could get very used to this lifestyle, Alex."

"I could too, Kacee," I said softly.

Chapter 28

We arrived at the hotel in time to shower, change, and get going to the show. Anthony was waiting for us downstairs, and he whisked us off to day two of this adventure. We arrived at the back entrance as we did the day before, and the cars were lined up as far as you could see to drop off models, designers, and anyone involved with this production. Anthony put the car in park and got out to open our door. He extended his hand to assist myself and Kacee out of the car. We both thanked him and walked into the back corridor. I looked up to see a familiar face walking towards us smiling.

"Good morning, ladies," Stephon said.

"Good morning to you, too," Kacee and I said at the same time.

"I trust you had an enjoyable evening with my parents last night?" he asked.

"Yes, we did," Kacee answered.

"And did my mother prepare a huge meal due to the fact that she was starving to death?" he asked, with a broadening smile on his face. We all laughed, and I shook my head yes.

"The meal was amazing and the hospitality was more than we could have imagined," I said. "We even ended up spending the night there."

"You did, did you?" Stephon asked with raised eyebrows and a devilish grin. I looked at him quizzically, and he laughed. "Ms. Alex, Ms. Kacee, that may have seemed unintentional, but I assure you, my parents had that planned out. They wanted to get to know you, and my father wanted one-on-one time with you. You see Ms. Alex, my father goes to great lengths when he sees great potential in designers. He takes the time to get to know them and takes it upon himself to give them insight and share his wisdom."

"Stephon, I am humbled and excited by your father's interest in our fashions, and very much look forward to working with him in the future." We both smiled at each other, and Stephon extended his arms to escort Kacee and me to the auditorium.

We walked in and took our third-row seats and anxiously waited for the show to begin. In no time at all the emcee took the stage and the show was underway. The models looked so graceful and strong on the catwalk, their movements were confident, and this year's fashions were over the top, showcasing the talents of their designers and the incredibly hard-working staff behind each stitch of clothing. I smiled as I thought about my hard-working staff who make Excellence Fashion House look so good. We had accomplished so much in such a short time with Kacee and me at the helm. I was very thankful for the opportunity that Mr. Elwin had given to me, for hiring me so many years ago, for selling me the company name and rights when the fashion house caught fire, and thanks to him, I now sat in Paris, watching the most cutting edge designs by the biggest names in fashion, and knowing my designs were seen by world renowned artists. I was once again humbled and honored to be included in this experience.

I looked at Kacee, who was so deep in thought, taking notes, and snapping photos that again I realized it wasn't just me here. It was my entire team and my family standing with me, and for that I had to bow my head and give thanks to God, for it was truly through his blessings that I had made it this far.

Chapter 28

I felt Kacee's hand on my arm. "Are you okay?" she asked.

I smiled and nodded, "Yes, I am more than fine." We both went back to watching the show and going back and forth over comments regarding a certain look, a certain style, and our likes and dislikes about a certain garment. Both of us realized it was such an accomplishment to even be here.

The show lasted another two hours or so, but the time just seemed to fly by. It was hard to determine which went faster: doing the walking on the runway or watching it from the sidelines. This had been such an experience that when the lights came up I was almost sad. I realized there was still another day of this fashion exhibit, but tomorrow would be the buying part of this trip.

I had always enjoyed the business part of these shows. I was the one doing the buying and working out the logistics of each item, but now that I had had a taste of the design side, I really kind of liked it.

Kacee and I rose from our seats and began to make our way to the reception area. It was time for some champagne and to get our times for the next day. Each buyer has an allotted amount of time with each fashion house representative, and that is what the next day would be all about. We received our times as potential buyers and we also received our area for the potential buyers to come to us. Since we had presented our line as well, the next day would be a very long day as we went from buyer to seller.

Kacee and I enjoyed our champagne, yet more than anything, we were looking forward to the meet and greet with such big names in the fashion industry. The excitement that was generated throughout the venue was almost intoxicating. Knowing that we stood there with the greatest in the fashion industry, conversing like we were lifetime friends and taking about what the future held was exhilarating to say the very least! As the meet and greet began to wind down and all of us were gathering our folders, an announcement came over the loud speaker. It was Jacquez himself, thanking everyone for this year's lines, for coming from around the world to be a part of this wonderful experience, welcoming the newly invited designers, and telling us to have a wonderful evening. Kacee and I finished gathering our stuff and made our way to the back exit where Anthony was waiting for us.

Anthony opened the door to our limo, and with a smile on his face motioned for us to get in. Kacee and I both said thank you and climbed into the limo. Anthony closed the door behind us, got in the driver's seat and asked, "How did your day go?"

"It was amazing, Anthony," I said with the voice of a school girl who had just been asked to prom. We all laughed and Anthony pulled out into traffic. "How was your day, Anthony?" I asked.

He looked at me and grinned. "It was good, Ms. Alex. Thank you for asking."

"What did you do today?" I asked.

"Well," Anthony started, "I try to spend as much time with my granddaughter as I can, and today she had a half day of school, so I picked her up in the limo and took her to the park so we could swing on the swings."

I smiled warmly at Anthony and said, "That is wonderful! I assume you took her for ice cream afterwards?" I asked with a little grin on my face.

Anthony looked at me in the rear-view mirror and smiled. "She does not like ice cream; she has to

190

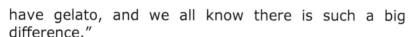

have gelato, and we all know there is such a big difference."

We all laughed and at that point I realized with how busy we had been. I hadn't spoken to my daughter or my husband. I found my phone in my purse and waited for someone at home to answer. "That's odd," I said out loud, "its 5:00 pm and no one is answering at home."

Kacee and Anthony looked at me and laughed. I looked at them both and asked, "What?"

Kacee said, "You must be tired! How long were we on the plane getting here?"

"I don't remember. Several hours, I know," I said.

"Well..." Kacee said, "If it takes several hours to get here, doesn't that tell you something?"

I looked at Kacee and then at Anthony and said, "Ahhh...." I shook my head. "Yes, I must be tired, duh.. Meghan is in school and Oliver is at work."

Both Kacee and Anthony busted out laughing, and I looked at them with that mean mommy look. Kacee looked out her window and Anthony just looked ahead, but both continued to snicker at me.

"Rotten children...both of you," I said then I snickered myself.

I dialed Oliver's cell, and he picked it up on the first ring. "Hey, Alex. How's it going honey," he asked.

"Oliver, it has been such a great experience. I am so glad we are here. How is Meghan?" I asked. "I miss you both so much, but we will be home soon. We wrap up the business end tomorrow then fly back the following day. Did Meghan have any homework? I know she has a spelling bee coming up, and she was a little nervous about it."

"Yes, Mommy, she had homework, and yes, I helped her with it." Oliver laughed. "She is doing great on her spelling and will be ready for the bee on Friday," he said.

"That works out great. I will be home late Thursday, so I will be able to go watch her on Friday," I said. "Are you going to be able to be there, Oliver?" I asked.

"Yes, I am taking Friday afternoon off so we can all spend the rest of the day together," he said.

"Oh that sounds wonderful! I have to go, dear. We are approaching our hotel. Tell Meghan I love her and I will call her tomorrow. Love you both," I said.

"I will tell her, and we love you too," Oliver said. We were hanging up just as Anthony was pulling the car up to the hotel door.

Anthony got out and opened the door for Kacee and me and extended his hand to assist us with getting out of the car.

"You know, Anthony," Kacee said, "We could certainly get used to this service. Do you treat everyone this way?"

"Ms. Kacee, I treat people with kindness and respect unless they give me a reason not to," he answered.

"You are one of a kind, Anthony," I said, "And I am grateful you have taken such good care of us."

"It's my pleasure, ladies. Is there anywhere else you would like for me to take you this evening?" he asked.

I looked at him with a smile on my face and said, "No, we kept you out late last night. We wouldn't do that to you two nights in a row."

"It was my pleasure, ladies. I will see you in the morning at 8 am." Anthony tipped his hat and got back in the limo and drove off.

Kacee and I walked into the hotel where we were greeted by the concierge. "Good evening, ladies. How was the show today?" he asked.

"It was excellent," Kacee answered.

"That is wonderful," he said. "Is there anything I can do for you ladies? Dinner reservations? Menus for room service? Spa appointments?" He asked.

I looked at Kacee and asked, "Where do you want to eat dinner?"

She looked at me and said, "You know, room service sounds good to me. How about you?"

"I think that sounds great. Could we have room service menus please?" I asked.

"Of course. Let me grab them for you," he said.

We took our menus and headed for the elevator door. We rode up in silence, and once inside our suite, Kacee and I both kicked off our shoes and went to our rooms to change clothes. There is nothing like the feeling of getting into your comfy clothes after a long day and feeling your body start to relax. It had been a fantastic day, and even though it had seemed to fly by, it had still been a long day. It was nice to just sit and relax for the evening.

We ordered room service and Kacee made us some tea while we waited for our food to arrive. Even though we were dining in, there was still a lot of work to be completed before tomorrow's purchasing day. Kacee and I gathered up our folders and notes and I began the process of deciding what lines I would purchase, what the cost sales ratio was, and what our projected profits would be. Kacee was excellent in her area of our business, but this part was mine, and we both knew that.

As we were discussing the clothing lines, there was a knock at our door. Dinner had arrived. "I am starving!" Kacee said. We looked at each other and laughed, both of us thinking of Camarra at that moment.

"Kacee," I said, "Please send Jacquez and Camarra flowers and wine from Excellence Fashions tomorrow, thanking them for their more than gracious hospitality.

"It's already done, Alex. The gifts are being delivered to their home tomorrow," Kacee said.

"Thanks, Kacee. You're the best!' I said.

We spent the rest of the evening going over every aspect of what the next day would bring: what lines we would be picking up and producing, what lines of our own would be sold, and the projections of the next year's inventory and profit. I read and reread the numbers, I don't know how many times, before we called it a night, and once I had gotten into bed I couldn't help but smile. As I said my prayers, I thanked God for the blessings he had given to me. This had been an amazing couple of days, and it was only through His Grace that I was here to be a part of all of this.

I reached for the phone to call home but thought the better of it. I was tired and at that moment I could not grasp the time difference, so I sent love from my heart to my husband and daughter, and with that I closed my eyes and drifted off to sleep. I don't think I even bothered to turn over I was so tired. I laughed at myself as I woke up in the same position I had gone to sleep in.

Chapter 29

Kacee came into my room with a hot cup of coffee in her hand, and I reached for the cup with a thank you on my face. She laughed at me and said, "This isn't for you. Get up and get ready. This is mine."

"You, Kacee, are a horrible person," I said while laughing.

"Yes I am," she laughed, "Now get ready. Anthony will be here in twenty minutes."

"Twenty minutes!" I squealed. "What time is it?" I reached for my watch, but knew that wouldn't matter with the time difference, so I ran to the shower and got myself ready for the day.

Anthony was waiting for us as we walked out the hotel entrance, and with a tip of his hat he opened the door and assisted us with getting into the limo. He closed the door behind us and got into the driver's seat, looked up in the rear-view mirror and said, "Good morning, ladies. There is fresh orange juice and blueberry scones for you if you would like," and with that he put the car in gear and headed for the event.

"Thank you, Anthony. This is wonderful," I said.

Kacee looked to Anthony and asked, "Do you treat all of your passengers this well, Anthony?"

"Only the ones I like, Ms. Kacee," he said with a smile and a wink.

We both smiled at him and looked out the windows of the car. Kacee and I were both excited about the day, but to be honest, I think I was ready for it to be over with so we could spend some time taking in the views of Paris. We arrived at the venue, but this time Anthony pulled to the front of the building, which made Kacee and I look at each other with a quizzical look.

Anthony saw the looks on our faces and said, "Today, ladies, you walk the red carpet. There will be photographers everywhere snapping photos of the designers, and your faces are about to go global. This is how stars are born and you have now reached worldwide notoriety. Enjoy it, and my advice to you both is, walk slowly." Anthony smiled and got out of the car to open our door and extended his hand.

The cameras were everywhere, just as Anthony said they would be. The rush that hit me was exhilarating, to say the very least, and I was pretty sure I was walking on a cloud. Just as we reached the front entrance, our names and our fashion house were announced over the loud speaker. We were then told to turn around for the cameras. There were a lot of flashes from the cameras and a lot of people shouting our names asking us to turn towards them for a picture. The flashes were almost blinding, and it was 10:00 am. We waved and smiled at the photographers, and then the door was opened for us and we were greeted inside by Stephon.

"Good morning, ladies. Nice to see you survived your first Paris red carpet," he said with a slight smile on his face. "You did survive, didn't you?" Stephon asked with yet another slight smile.

"Yes, we did. Thank you, Stephon," I giggled as I answered. I looked at Stephon and said, "You know, I have been to many fashion shows, but have never walked the red carpet to the entrance."

"Ah, but you have not been to THE fashion show in Paris, now have you?" Stephon laughed.

"No. No, I have not," I said.

Chapter 29

♥♥♥♥♥♥♥♥♥♥♥♥

Stephon escorted us to the reception area and kissed us both on the cheeks as he walked away. "Enjoy, ladies. It as has been a pleasure to meet both of you," he said softly.

"Thank you, Stephon, for everything," I said. Kacee had already gone to prepare our folders for the purchasing part of today, then she would prepare the folders for the selling part. All the work we had done last night had led us up to this moment for this day. It was exciting, and this was going to go fast, so we both knew it was time to bring our A game and make our final decisions.

The hours flew by as we procured our newest lines and sold our lines as well. The connections we were making, the product we were buying, and the lines we were selling made for a very productive day, and by the time late afternoon arrived we had completed what we had set out to accomplish.

As we were gathering up our folders, Jacquez came walking up to us. "Ms. Alex, Ms. Kacee," he said, "I hope you have had a wonderful time here and I hope to see you again next year. Thank you for the lovely gifts that arrived at our home today, but you did not need to do that. It was our pleasure to get to know the both of you, and Alex, I look forward to hearing from you anytime. Enjoy your trip home to the States." With that, Jacquez lifted my hand and kissed it.

"Thank you, Jacquez. The pleasure has been all mine," I said. Jacquez kissed Kacee on the cheek and walked away.

I looked at Kacee, who was staring at me. "What?" I asked. "Why are you looking at me like that?"

Kacee arched that eyebrow and said, "Uh huh," and began to walk towards the door.

"What, uh huh?" I asked. "What do you mean, uh huh?" I asked again while I giggled like a school girl. I hadn't paid attention to the fact that there was a small piece of paper in my hand until it fell to the floor. I reached to pick it up and realized Jacquez had given me his personal cell number and a short note telling me to call him anytime. Kacee watched me stuff it quickly into my pocket but didn't ask what it was. I think she already knew.

We walked outside to find Anthony once again waiting for us. He tipped his hat and opened our door for us. "Ladies?" he asked, "Where would you like to go? Back to your hotel, or maybe an early dinner, or sightseeing maybe?"

I looked at Anthony and said, "We had planned on taking in some of the highlights of Paris tomorrow, but if you have time, Anthony, I can't think of a better tour guide than you. So please, show us the beautiful city of Paris," I said and smiled. Anthony nodded his head and began to narrate as he drove us all over the grand city. We stopped at several places and even took in a little shopping here and there. We even got Anthony to go in some of the boutiques with us.

Kacee and I both laughed at him when we went into the fragrance store; the look on his face was priceless. "How do you ladies ever pick a scent in a place like this?" he asked. "My wife wears the same wonderful smelling perfume that she wore the day we met," Anthony said with a huge smile on his face.

"How long have you been married, Anthony?" I asked.

"We have been married for 45 years, and I consider myself the luckiest man alive to have her."

Chapter 29

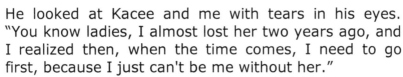

He looked at Kacee and me with tears in his eyes. "You know ladies, I almost lost her two years ago, and I realized then, when the time comes, I need to go first, because I just can't be me without her."

"Oh, Anthony, that is probably the most beautiful thing I have ever heard. Now stop, or we will all be crying," I joked. He wiped his eyes and walked us back to the limo. "Anthony, I know today is our last day with your service, but I want you to know something. We are fortunate to have met you during this wonderful adventure and look forward to staying in touch with you and your family always," I said as my eyes misted up yet another time.

"Ms. Alex," he said, "the pleasure has been all mine." Anthony drove us back to the hotel and wished us a good evening, then drove off.

Kacee looked at me and said, "Are you ready for dinner? I am starving," she said.

"Yes, I am hungry too," I said. We decided we would go to our suite and dress for dinner. It wasn't often Kacee and I dressed up this much, but when in Rome...*but wait we are in France, not Rome* I laughed to myself. We dressed to the nines and called for a car to take us to the dinner theater that Kacee had made our reservations with this morning. It was obviously the place to be, because the place was packed. The show was about to begin as we were escorted to our seats. The lights slowly dimmed and the music began to fill the theater. The wait staff brought our drinks and dinner was served while the show was being performed. It was one of the greatest presentations I had ever seen. As the lights were coming back up the applause erupted to almost deafening levels.

Kacee and I were on our feet as well, with the rest of the theater, applauding and cheering. The lights slowly dimmed, and once again we took our seats as our dessert was being served. We sat there enjoying our amazing dessert and enjoying some of the best coffee I had ever had in my life as the vocals faded to violins, and the lights came back up in the theater. It truly was a perfect ending to a long and yet very productive day. Kacee and I smiled at each other as we rose from our seats. We walked in silence as we followed the masses outside to the car that would take us back to our hotel.

"You know, Kacee," I said, "This has been one of the most incredible experiences of my life." Kacee nodded her head, but never said a word.

When we arrived back at the hotel, the concierge met us asking if there was anything we needed. "No, we are fine," I answered. He smiled and walked us to the elevator.

Kacee and I walked into our suite and both of us headed for our rooms to change. Yes, it had been a wonderful day, but we were both ready for comfy clothes, and to sit on the balcony and gaze at the stars and the lights of this breathtaking city. We had sat there for several minutes when my phone rang and about made me jump out of my seat. Kacee laughed at me and headed back into the suite.

"Hey, Honey. How is everything going?" I asked.

"We are good, Sweetheart," he said. "Meghan and I were missing you, so we had to call."

I smiled and said, "I am happy you did. I have been missing you both too." I could hear Meghan in the background, and I knew I needed to hear about her day and what she had been up to. I realized at that moment that Paris was great, but that little girl and that man are what made my life complete.

Chapter 29

♥ ♥ ♥ ♥ ♥ ♥ ♥ ♥ ♥ ♥ ♥ ♥ ♥

Oliver tried to talk, but Meghan was not having it. All I could hear was, "Let me talk to Mommy, let me talk to Mommy." I laughed and told Oliver to put her on the phone. "Hi, Mommy!" Meghan squealed. "I miss you, Mommy. When are you coming home?" she asked.

"Well little girl, we will be on a plane tomorrow headed home," I said.

"I have missed you so much," Meghan said.

"I have missed you more, little one," I answered back to her.

"No, Mommy, I have missed you more," she said. Then she told me all about her day, her homework, and how she wants a puppy.

"A puppy, huh?" I asked. "Well, we will all discuss that when I get home, okay?"

"Okay, Mommy. I love you and I have to go now. Daddy wants the phone." Before I could even say goodbye to her Oliver was back on the phone.

"Hey, lady," he said.

"Hey babe. Sounds like Meghan is great, but what is this about a puppy?" I asked.

"Well, Emy got a puppy, so Meghan thinks she needs to have one." Oliver laughed. "She actually told me how caring for a puppy would make her a more responsible adult."

"Oh, wow, that child is really probably more adult than I am at times," I said. Oliver and I both laughed.

"Yeah me too," he said. "What time does your flight get in tomorrow?" he asked.

"We will be landing at 4:45, so I am going to stop by the fashion house for a few, then come on home," I said. "I have missed both of you very much, and I am ready to be home and sleep in our bed," I said.

Oliver snickered, and said, "I don't how much sleep you will get. Meghan will probably talk your ear off most of the night, but I love hearing you say our bed."

"I love you, Oliver," I said.

"I love you too, Alex," he said, and we hung up.

I stared out at the lights like I was all but in a trance when I jumped up and yelled to Kacee, "Hey, did you know you have a puppy?" I laughed.

"Wait, what?" Kacee shouted. "Oh no, he did not let Emy have a puppy. We discussed this before we left to come to Paris," Kacee growled. "That man never listens to me...ugh!" Kacee rolled her eyes, and I couldn't help but laugh.

I was exhausted, and I know Kacee was too, so we decided to call it a night. I climbed into my bed and don't really remember closing my eyes. Before I knew it, it was time to wake up again. *Wow, that was a short night*, I thought, but I was excited to be heading home. I could hear Kacee stirring around, so I knew the coffee would be waiting for me after my shower. *I really am spoiled at times,* I thought to myself and laughed as I turned on the hot water. I dressed quickly and joined Kacee in the kitchen where my coffee was waiting for me on the table. "Thanks," I said to her.

Kacee smiled at me said, "Yes, you are spoiled." I laughed and had turned around to walk out on the balcony, but I turned around to look at her again with that how-did-you-know-what-I-was-thinking look. "I just know, Alex; that's how," Kacee whispered.

"Oh, that's not weird at all," I laughed. I enjoyed the spectacular view from our suite, but it

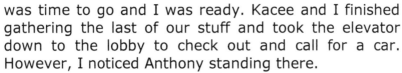

was time to go and I was ready. Kacee and I finished gathering the last of our stuff and took the elevator down to the lobby to check out and call for a car. However, I noticed Anthony standing there.

"Good morning, ladies," Anthony said.

"Good morning, Anthony," we both said in unison. "Are you picking up someone this morning?" I asked.

"As a matter of fact, I am," Anthony said, "If you ladies will follow me, your car is waiting for you."

Kacee looked at me with a quizzical look on her face. I shrugged my shoulders and followed Anthony to the car. Anthony opened the door and assisted us into the car and closed the door behind us. "Anthony?" I asked, "I thought yesterday was the last day you would be driving us.

There is fresh orange juice and muffins waiting for you ladies if you would like," Anthony said as he winked at us and pulled the car into traffic.

"Thank you, Anthony. This is so nice of you," I said.

"Ms. Alex," Anthony said, "It has been my pleasure to get to know both of you ladies, and I wanted to make sure you got to your plane safely this morning. Jacquez felt the same way. You ladies made quite an impression on him and took this year's show by storm. Paris may never be the same after you leave," Anthony said with a big grin on his face.

We arrived at the airport and were given curb service, thanks to Anthony. He stopped the limo at the main entrance, assisted us out of the car, and had a young man get our bags for us. "Thank you, Anthony, for everything," I said. "You truly made this a more than wonderful experience for both of us," Kacee said. Anthony extended his hand to shake mine, but when I gave him a hug, I got a quick squeeze in return from him too.

"Ladies," Anthony said as he tipped his hat and turned and walked away. I wasn't looking forward to the lengthy amount of time it would take to go through security, as the line was very long, but as we were standing there this young lady walked up to us and told us come with her. Kacee and I looked at each other with a bit of a nervous look but followed as instructed. We walked to the side of the metal detector and through a door that led us to the other side of the check in counter.

The lady took our tickets and stamped them and told us we were ready to go to Concourse 12, where we could board our plane. The look on my face must have said it all, because she looked at me and said, "I saw you on the news and researched your line and loved it. I am officially of fan of Excellence Fashion House. I already placed an order for the sea breeze suit, and I can't wait for it to get here," she said excitedly.

"Thank you so much for liking and ordering our designs. We look forward to having you as a customer for many years to come." I said.

"I will be!" she said and motioned for us to continue down to where we would be boarding.

Kacee and I looked at each other like a couple of school girls and giggled. Once we arrived at our concourse, the attendant stamped our tickets and we were allowed to board the plane. No one else had boarded yet, so Kacee and I took our time making our way to our seats and getting our carry-ons in the overhead compartment. The flight attendant asked if there was anything we wanted or needed. "No, I believe we are fine, thank you," I said.

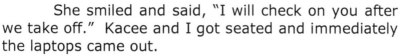
She smiled and said, "I will check on you after we take off." Kacee and I got seated and immediately the laptops came out.

This had been such a successful trip that I felt that Excellence Fashion House was catapulted to the next level. I knew Excellence Fashions was ready for this, but I wasn't sure if I was. Kacee and I worked tirelessly on the flight back home, taking a few breaks here and there to stretch our legs and look out the window. The sun peeked in and out of the clouds for most of the flight, but we did get to see a spectacular sunset as we were waiting to land.

Kacee and I had discussed running by the fashion house on the way home for just a quick check in, but we both knew that we would not be capable of doing that and decided to go home instead. We picked up our luggage at baggage claim and made our way to the car. Kacee's husband had picked up her car from the fashion house, so I dropped her off at her house. Emy must have been watching from the window because just as I pulled in the driveway, the front door flew open and Emy was running to jump in her mommy's arms. "Mommy, Mommy, Mommy!" Emy screamed with excitement, wrapping her arms around Kacee's neck. "I missed you so much, Mommy. I am so glad you are home," Emy squealed.

"I am glad to be home too Emy," Kacee said as she tried to put her down to reach her suitcase, but Emy was not having it.

"Oh, no, Mommy. Please don't let go of me. I have missed you too much," Emy said.

I looked at Kacee and smiled. "I got your luggage; meet you inside," I said. Emy was talking a mile a minute when I walked into the kitchen, and

Kacee's husband had that look on his face that said, "Your turn!"

I couldn't help but giggle a bit and set the suitcase down. I waved goodbye to everyone so as not to interrupt Emy and made my way out the door to my car. I couldn't help but smile on the way home, thinking about this last week. The trip was amazing. There were no other words that came to mind, but the greatest thing I saw was Emy holding onto her mommy so tightly and telling her how much she loved and missed her. I couldn't wait to get home to my family and enjoy the same type of welcome home reception.

I pulled into the driveway expecting Meghan to fly out the door to greet me, but she did not. I was somewhat disappointed to not see anyone waiting for me outside. Oliver's car was in the garage, so I knew they were home, yet no one came outside to greet me. I grabbed my suitcases and made my way up the sidewalk, juggling my purse, laptop, luggage and gifts. When I reached the door, I fumbled for my keys, got the door unlocked and walked into a very quiet house. I have to be honest; at that point I was a bit concerned. The television wasn't on, Meghan wasn't running around anywhere, and I didn't hear anything but silence. I walked into the kitchen and flipped on the light to hear Meghan yell, "Surprise Mommy!" "Happy Birthday, Mommy!"

There she stood with a cake in her hands trying desperately not to drop it on the floor, with the biggest smile I had ever seen. I took the cake from her hands and set it on the table. Then I saw Oliver outside at the grill. He looked at me and almost ran into the house. "Meghan," he said, "You were

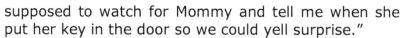

supposed to watch for Mommy and tell me when she put her key in the door so we could yell surprise."

Meghan looked at him and said, "I did say surprise, just like you said to, Daddy." I looked at Oliver and laughed.

"Well, she did say surprise," I said to him. We all laughed and hugged each other. Meghan was in my arms in a blink of an eye and Oliver had his arms around us.

Oliver looked at me and said, "Get ready for dinner. I made your favorite." Meghan followed me to the powder room and washed for dinner with me. Meghan, like Emy, was talking a mile a minute, and I loved every second of this. We went outside to the patio where the evening lights were lit up and candles were on the table. It was absolutely perfect; the company was the best part, but I have to admit the food was pretty awesome too. Oliver had outdone himself. After dinner, they sang Happy Birthday to me and we enjoyed the cake that the two of them had made for me. We were sitting there talking and laughing and enjoying the cake and presents when I couldn't help but bust out laughing. "What is it, Mommy? Why are you laughing?" Meghan asked.

"I totally forgot today was my birthday, Meghan. How silly is that?" I asked her.

Meghan looked at me and laughed, "Mommy, I would never forget your birthday, so if you don't remember it I will always remember for you."

I smiled at her with tears in my eyes. "Thank you, baby girl," I said. "That is the sweetest thing I have ever heard," I whispered.

This was undoubtedly the best birthday I had ever had. We spent the remaining hours of the evening discussing the events of the past week, from school, to work, to baths, and I truly think we covered every topic known to exist. Oliver and I walked Meghan to her room where he tucked her in as I read her a night time story. I just kept thinking to myself that my family was the greatest blessing that God had given to me. I knew I was never going to be able to say thank you enough to show my appreciation for His love. I finished reading and put the book down to find both Oliver and Meghan asleep. I softly woke Oliver, and we closed the door behind us on our way out. Oliver turned and asked if I wanted some coffee. I shook my head no and reached for his hand. It had been a long day, a long flight, and a wonderful evening, but I was ready to climb into our bed and fall asleep in my husband's arms, and that's pretty much what happened.

I was awakened the next morning from a very sound sleep by something that smelled too good to not go investigate. I walked down the stairs to find Oliver and Meghan both staring in the oven like it was a movie screen. I snickered a bit and Meghan turned and said to me so grown-up like, "Well, good morning sleepy head, or should I say good afternoon?"

"Well good morning to you too little missy," I said as I smiled and winked at her. "What time is it?" I asked.

"It is 12:30, so actually it is afternoon," Meghan replied.

"You two let me sleep in this late?" I asked in shock. "And what is that amazing smell coming from the oven?" I asked.

"Well," Oliver said, "Meghan and I have been working on a breakfast bake, and I am pretty sure we have now perfected it.

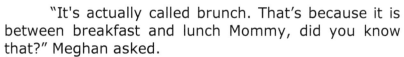

"It's actually called brunch. That's because it is between breakfast and lunch Mommy, did you know that?" Meghan asked.

"Well, little one, when did you get so smart?" I asked.

"Last week," Meghan replied without as much as a glance at Oliver or me. We both looked at each other and grinned.

"Meghan if you will get the plates, I will get the napkins and silverware, while Daddy takes that wonderful smelling food out of the oven, and we will sit down to a wonderful brunch as a family," I smiled and said.

"Okay, Mommy," Meghan said. We sat down at the table and bowed our heads to give thanks to God for the many blessings he had bestowed upon this family, and Oliver dished up the casserole. I put the fruit on the plates, and Meghan passed around the jelly. We were like a little assembly line, and all the workers did their jobs excellently, I thought to myself. We enjoyed our meal and the company was even better.

As we cleared the table and loaded the dishwasher, Meghan looked at Oliver and whispered, loudly, "Can we tell her yet, Daddy?"

Oliver put his finger to his lips and whispered, "Shhh! No, not yet Meghan."

"Tell me what?" I asked. Both of them pretended like they didn't hear me and went along with their business. "Okay, you two," I said with my eyebrow raised, "What are you planning?"

"Now, Daddy?" Meghan asked.

"Okay, Meghan. Yes, now."

Meghan screeched and grabbed my hand. "Come on, Mommy, we have a birthday surprise for you." We all but ran into the living room where there was a very large box with a big pink bow on top. I looked at the two of them, and both were grinning from ear to ear.

"You two! You gave me my presents last night, and today there is more?" I asked.

Oliver put his arms around me, "Alex, you have been working so hard these last couple of months, with your career and taking care of us, that we wanted to show you how much we love and appreciate you. Last night you were dead on your feet, so you needed a good night's sleep and a good breakfast this morning so that we could officially celebrate your birthday."

I stood there feeling so complete and happy that it didn't really matter to me what was in the box, but Meghan was so excited I pulled the ribbon off the box and opened it to find several smaller boxes inside, all with pink ribbons.

"Well, you two must have taken a great amount of time to make these boxes look so pretty. I almost hate to open them."

I grinned a little grin at Oliver as we both were watching Meghan, who was about to jump out of her skin with excitement. Meghan looked at me so seriously and softly whispered, "Mommy, the presents are inside the boxes, not the boxes themselves."

I looked at her and said, "Oh, okay. How silly of me, Meghan. Thanks for explaining that to me."

"No problem, Mommy. I am here to help," she said with a huge smile on her face. I opened the boxes to find a beautiful sapphire necklace and matching earrings, a huge box of chocolates, a gift card to the day spa, and a new briefcase. I noticed the envelope at the bottom of the box but something told me to wait on that for a minute or two.

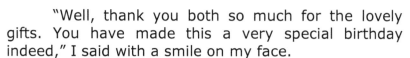

"Well, thank you both so much for the lovely gifts. You have made this a very special birthday indeed," I said with a smile on my face.

Meghan looked up at Oliver with a very puzzled look on her face and motioned for him to bend down to her. She whispered in to his ear, rather loudly, "Daddy did you forget to put the envelope in the box?"

"Well Meghan, I think I put it in there, better have Mommy look again."

Meghan looked at me and said, "Mommy, are you sure you found everything in that box?"

"Well honey, let me look again," so I looked down and reached for the envelope that was in the bottom. "Wait. I do see something else in here. What could this be?" I asked Meghan.

"It's a surprise, Mommy, open it!" she squealed.

I opened the envelope and couldn't help myself. "Well, there are three tickets to the puppet show at the library. That is wonderful," I said with a big smile on my face. "Thank you again so much, you two," I said, almost laughing at the look of bewilderment on Meghan's face.

Meghan looked at me and then at her father, and said so maturely, "Okay, I don't understand. Something has gone terribly wrong with this gift thing."

Oliver and I looked at each other and grinned, both of us trying not to laugh out loud. "Meghan?" Oliver asked, "Don't you want to take Mommy to the puppet show at the library?"

"To be honest, Daddy, I don't really like puppets, so if you and Mommy want to go on a date there, you can leave me with Mrs. Sigel please."

That was it, I couldn't hold back the laughter anymore, Meghan looked at me again with that what is wrong with that woman face, and I pulled her close to me and said, "Thank you for the tickets to Disneyland sweet girl. I can't wait to go."

The look on her face was shock and happiness, "Oh Mommy, you found the right tickets!" Meghan screeched.

"Yes baby, I found the right tickets. We are going to Disney," I smiled and said.

I don't think Meghan's feet touched the ground, she was so excited. She ran all over the house and then stopped dead in her tracks. "Mommy, are we going today?"

"Why do you ask, Meghan?" "Well, if we are, we need to go shopping first. I don't have a thing to wear, she said as she ran up the stairs. I laughed so hard that I was actually crying. *Oh, that child* I thought to myself.

Oliver came and sat beside me, "You really had her going on the tickets Alex. Poor kid. I thought she was going to lose her mind for a minute," he laughed

"I thought so too hon," I said to him. We both laughed and spent the rest of the day making plans for our trip, playing in the pool with Meghan and enjoying this perfect day. Oliver woke us up the next morning to tell me we'd better hurry or we would be late for Mass. We all scurried around and made it with time to spare. I sat there and listened to the Gospel being read and couldn't help but feel it was meant for me and my family today. *We are blessed, and God has a plan for each of us, and that is what was going through my head. I understand more and more every day. It's not my will; it's God's will; not my time, but God's time. I get it now.* I smiled and thought to myself.

The years were passing by quickly, and our lives had gotten even busier with every passing day. We had always been active in our church, Meghan was in everything in school, the success of the fashion house was beyond my highest expectations and Oliver now served as the Administrator over policy and procedures for the regional hospital authority board. Many times I bowed my head and thanked God for his many blessings. We spent many long weekends at the cabin as a family, occasionally taking one of Meghan's friends along as well. Sometimes Oliver and I had to realize that our daughter was growing up and we were not the center of her world, like she was ours. The time was now here for high school graduation, and Meghan graduated with honors as we knew she would. She had burnt the midnight oil many, many times, and she was now going to see the fruits of her labors. Oliver hoped she would follow in his footsteps and get her degree in business, from his alma mater, and I just wanted her to be happy. Yes, a part of me wanted her to follow in my footsteps as well, but we both new that whatever field she chose, she would be exceptional. Oliver and I had agreed that when the letter of acceptance came, it was time to buy our daughter a new car. Although we did insist Meghan do her very best in school, which she did, she also worked summers at the fashion house to make sure she understood the value of hard work and often long hours. Meghan was a hard-working young lady and her father and I both took pride in her work ethic and dedication, whether she was sweeping floors or walking the runway we were proud of her. Excellence Fashions took us all over the world and the connections we had made so many years ago now were ones that were still important to us as we were to them.

Upon hearing of our daughter's soon approaching graduation, gifts came in from all over the world. We did receive a surprise when Colt called to congratulate Meghan and invite us to his upcoming nuptials. I was very happy to hear he had made the decision to remarry after so long and share the rest of his life with a wonderful lady, and we visited for quite some time when Oliver got on the phone with him. "We would love to come, Colt," Oliver said. "We look forward to seeing you soon." "Well, what about that," Oliver smiled and said.

"Yes, I shook my head, what about that."

When Meghan got in from work, we could hear the screams of excitement from the driveway. "I got in!" she squealed over and over, "I got in!" Oliver opened the door to watch Meghan rush by him. "Mom!" she screamed. "I got in!" Meghan tried to show me the letter, but her hands were shaking from the excitement.

Oliver looked at her and laughed. "Mom, I got in?" he asked. "What about Dad, I got in?"

"Oh Daddy, I got in!" Meghan squealed.

"I kinda guessed that, sweetheart," he laughed.

Meghan ran upstairs to put her swim suit on in her room and call Emy. They had stayed best friends all though school, which made sense to me as Kacee and I were still best friends. Oliver and I went out to sit by the pool and I just couldn't help but know how blessed I had been. Oliver poured us some coffee as I sat down. "We did it, Alex. We got our daughter though high school," he said as he beamed with pride.

"Yes, we did. Now we just have to buy a car and pay college tuition," I laughed. "College tuition? Oliver, wait! She didn't tell us where she got into," I said quizzically. Meghan had applied to a couple of universities, so even though she got in, we had no idea where.

Oliver and I both busted out laughing as Meghan came outside to get in the pool. "What are you two laughing at?" Meghan asked.

Oliver stood up and walked to her, "Well, Miss I got in, you didn't tell your parents where you got in," Oliver said with a smirk on his face.

"Oh, I was so excited I forgot to tell you." Meghan laughed. "Here is my acceptance letter. Now I have to get in the pool for a swim before we go get my new car." Meghan laughed as she dove in, making sure she splashed her father and myself.

"Oh, you hoo do!" I laughed, acting like I was soaking wet. We watched Meghan play in the pool for a while. When Emy rang the doorbell, she had come to swim with Meghan and celebrate her good news. I told the girls we would be going out for dinner in about an hour so they could swim for a while and then get dressed. The girls enjoyed the water for some time. Oliver and I were getting dressed for dinner when the girls came in and ran upstairs to change. I thought to myself: *I have watched or heard that girl run up and down those steps a million times not realizing how fast the time was passing by*. I have often looked back wondering how my life would have been if Meghan hadn't come into it. *I am so proud of the young lady she has become, and her future is going to be amazing* I thought to myself.

I was standing there in kind of a daze when Oliver put his hand on my shoulder and woke me out of my thoughts. "Are you ready?" he asked. "You look beautiful, Alex," he said softly and kissed me on the cheek.

I smiled at him and nodded my head yes. We all piled into the car, and I counted, "One, two, and three."

"Where are we going to dinner?" Meghan asked.

I couldn't help but laugh to myself. Oliver looked at me and chuckled himself. All of that girl's life, once she had gotten in the car, she immediately asked where we were going. It didn't matter if we were going to the store, on a vacation, or just around the block, Meghan had to have a destination before we could leave the driveway. We have raised a young woman with a destination in front of her always.

"You will see in a few minutes," Oliver answered. "We have a quick stop to make, then we will be going to dinner."

Oliver didn't tell me where we were going, but my intuition told me it had something to do with four wheels. I couldn't help but smile when we pulled into the car lot. Meghan and Emy were so busy talking that she didn't even pay attention to where we were. Oliver looked at me and waited for the girls to stop talking. They went from mid-sentence to dead silence; then the squeal from Meghan's voice all but broke my eardrums. I did cover my ears and laugh as she jumped out of the car.

"Oh my gosh Daddy! Are you serious?"

"Yes, little girl, let's look at cars."

It didn't take a second for Meghan to run to the car she wanted. Oliver and I knew which one she would want but wanted her to pick it out. The young salesman came walking out of the showroom and made his way to us. "Hello there folks. My name is Robert. What can I show you today?"

Chapter 29

♥♥♥♥♥♥♥♥♥♥♥♥♥

"Well Robert," Oliver said, "we need the keys for this one."

"I just happen to have them in my hand, Oliver," Robert said with a smile and a wink.

Meghan couldn't wait to get behind the wheel, and like every teenager, the first thing to check out was the radio. I was standing there with Oliver talking with the young salesman when Meghan asked, "Can I take it for a spin now?"

I shook my head yes and Meghan yelled for Emy to get in the car with her.

"Be careful," Oliver and I said at the same time as the girls pulled off the lot.

I looked at Oliver and the young salesman and noticed they certainly favored in looks. I also couldn't help but notice they stood the same way. *It must be a guy thing* I thought, and I shrugged it off. I did mention to both of them that I noticed the smile and wink Robert gave to Oliver. Robert smiled and Oliver whispered to me, in a voice actually a bit louder than a whisper, "I stopped by here this week and picked out the car I knew she would want," Oliver said. "I have already completed the paperwork and it's hers to drive off the lot if she wants it."

"If she wants it?" I asked. I snickered at first but then I started to give it some thought and, I have to admit I didn't really like the fact that Oliver had made such a large purchase without talking to me about it, and even more oddly, I didn't notice any purchases that large coming out of our checking account. *I might forget to write down a debt here and there, but this is a car!* I thought to myself.

Meghan and Emy were pulling back into the car lot with huge smiles on both of their faces. It was more than obvious this was the car that Meghan wanted. Meghan parked the car carefully and got out. She slowly extended her hand towards Robert handing him the keys.

"Well?" Oliver asked.

"Well, Daddy, it's perfect and I love it! Can I have it?" Meghan asked sheepishly.

"You'd better ask your mom, just to be on the safe side, kiddo," Oliver said and grinned.

Meghan looked at me and before she could even say a word I shook my head yes. The screams of joy from Meghan and Emy were almost deafening. I covered my ears and laughed at them for being so loud. Meghan hugged me and her dad and Emy and would have probably hugged the car salesman, but when she squealed so loud, it kind of scared him and he backed up a good bit from her. I looked at Oliver and saw a strange look on his face. He was staring at the car salesman with a big grin on his face. It was like they knew each other or something, but again, maybe just a guy thing going on, I thought to myself.

"Okay, everyone!" I had to all but shout. "I am still hungry, so can we wrap this up please?" Oliver and Robert shook hands as Robert was thanking us for our business. "Okay, girls, meet us at Rae's for dinner. We have reservations and we are about to be late," I said.

Emy said, "That's one of my favorite places! Let's go, Meghan."

Meghan put the top down on her new car, fastened her seat belt, put her sunglasses on and drove off like she had been driving for years. Oliver and I were getting into the car to follow the girls to the restaurant when he looked at me and asked, "What is it, Alex? You have that look, the look that says you are pondering something."

"Well, Oliver, actually I am," I said and looked directly at him. "How did you pay for this car?"

"What do you mean how did I pay for this car?" Oliver asked me.

"I mean, how did you pay for this car? Was it with a check, a debit card, where did you get the money?" I asked.

Oliver was taken aback by the question I had just asked him, again, and took his time to answer me. "We have the money to buy our daughter a car, Alex. You were all excited about this too, so what is the issue, Alex?" Oliver asked in a harsh tone.

"I didn't say we couldn't afford it, and I didn't say I wasn't excited; I asked how you paid for it!" I snapped.

Oliver looked at me and said, "I wrote a check, that is how I paid for it."

"You wrote a check from our account?" I asked.

"Yes, from our account," he answered in a very annoyed voice.

"I see," I mumbled. "What day did you say you purchased this car, Oliver? And how much did you pay for the car?" I asked in an instantly calm voice.

"It was Thursday or Friday of last week and why do you want to know how much I paid?" Oliver asked in an irritated voice.

"Well, it's funny to me that I just balanced our checkbook like I do every month and there wasn't a check written for a car. I think I would have noticed a check for $36,000.00, and I can bet you that I would have come to you and asked what that was for and why this wasn't discussed with me prior to the purchase. But since the money didn't come out of our joint account, I have to question what account it did come out of."

"I knew you wouldn't have wanted to pay that much for her first car. And by the way, Alex, if you already knew how much I gave for it, why did you ask me? And how did you know that amount when I didn't tell you yet?" Oliver asked with a surprised look on his face.

"The amount was on the key chain. I saw it when that salesman handed the key over," I snapped. "So we have now established the amount you paid for the car, even though you didn't see fit to just tell me. What you still haven't told me is where the money came from."

We were pulling into Rae's parking lot when Oliver asked softly, "Can we talk about this when we get home please? I want Meghan to have a great evening and not know her parents are fighting over something as senseless as money," Oliver said with an edge in his voice.

"Sure, we can drop this for now, but rest assured we will be discussing this as soon as we get home."

With a little pat on Oliver's right hand I got out of the car. The restaurant was extremely busy and it seemed to take forever to get our drinks and dinner. The food was good and the girls' excitement made the evening very enjoyable. We all sat and talked like any other night, but tonight seemed different to me, not just due to the fact that I was upset with Oliver, but something just felt off. We enjoyed our dessert and Oliver went to pay as the girls and I headed for our cars. While we were outside Meghan asked if she could spend the night with Emy. I knew Oliver's and my discussion would pick up where it left off, so I told her it was fine. I told her to drive safe and text me when they got to Emy's house. Oliver came out of the

Chapter 29

♥ ♥ ♥ ♥ ♥ ♥ ♥ ♥ ♥ ♥ ♥ ♥

restaurant and began looking for Meghan's car. I put my window down and told him Meghan had gone to Emy's for the night. The look on his face was one of pure dread. I have to be honest, I wasn't feeling the love right that moment either. The drive home was silent and a different type of uncomfortable. Oliver and I were not used to arguing a lot, we always saw the opportunity to settle the issue and move on, but my gut told me that was not going to be the case tonight.

We pulled into the driveway and Oliver put the car in park, but didn't turn it off. I turned to look at him and saw anger in his eyes. "Are you going to turn the car off, or are you going somewhere?" I asked.

Oliver turned the car off and looked at me. "No Alex, I am not going anywhere, but we do need to talk."

I felt my very inside go cold and I realized I had felt this feeling before, but it had been many years ago and I knew this would not be an easy night. We walked up the sidewalk and Oliver opened the door for me as he always did. Once inside he took my jacket and his, hung them up in the hallway and walked directly past me to the living room and sat down. I followed him to the doorway where I stood and stared at him. He patted the couch for me to come sit beside him but I did not move, I just stood there watching him, waiting for this, whatever this was, to start. "Okay, Oliver, let's get this out in the open. Where did the money come from to buy Meghan's car?" I asked. "I know it didn't come out of our joint account and now my gut tells me there is another account that I know nothing about. Is that true Oliver?"

Oliver didn't answer, just sat there with his head bowed down.

"Oliver, you need to answer me. You need to start talking," I said in a demanding voice.

"Alexandra," Oliver said, "for many years we have been putting money in our checking and our savings accounts, and we have a very very comfortable amount of money. If we didn't put another dime in it we could live very well for the rest of our lives."

"I am aware of that Oliver. That was kind of the plan. We were to enjoy our life together, raise our daughter, work hard and be successful in our careers. That is what I have been doing for the last 20 plus years; what have you been doing?" I asked in a shaky voice.

"Alexandra, about 15 years ago I opened my own savings account, and every month I have been putting money aside for..."

"For what?" I cut him off. "Why do you have a private savings account? Am I on it with you?" I asked.

"No, you aren't. I put Meghan on it when she turned 12, but she doesn't know anything about it." Oliver said softly.

"Oliver, I am confused. Why would you do this? Why would you keep this kind of secret from me? Is this where the money from the car came from?" I know the questions were coming out quicker than he could answer, but they just kept coming out of my mouth. "Oliver, what is it that you really need to tell me? Yes, I am upset about the private bank account, and by the way how much do you have in there?" I asked while tapping my foot.

Oliver raised his head and looked at me, "I have just over three million dollars in that account, Alex."

♥ ♥ ♥ ♥ ♥ ♥ ♥ ♥ ♥ ♥ ♥ ♥ ♥ ♥

"Three million dollars, Oliver? Are you kidding me? Why am I not on the account with you? Why is there an account?"

Again the questions began to flood out of my mouth. Oliver stood up and began to walk closer to me. "Oh, no, you don't," I said as I took a couple steps backward. "We've done this before. I won't and can't go through this the rest of my life with your secrets popping up every so many years. Oliver, I can see there is something you need to tell me, and I know you well enough by now to see in your eyes you don't want to tell me, but you'd better start talking and you'd better do it now!"

Oliver stood there, took a deep breath and started talking. "Alexandra, you are the love of my life, and the only reason this marriage is ending is because of me. I found out about 11 years ago that I had a son and his name is Robert. I knew after what I had put you through with Meghan that I could not do this to you again. I started putting money back for him the day I found out about him. One of the differences between Meghan and Robert is that Robert's father, the man who raised him, did not know that Robert was not his biological child. The man passed away and it wasn't until his passing that Robert found out about me. Robert grew up in a loving family with two wonderful parents and was very angry and shocked by all of this, so when his mother contacted me, I wanted to do whatever I could to help him and get to know him too. Like Robert, I was very upset and angry that I had a son and had missed so much of his life due to her lies."

"Wait. Due to her lies?" I asked with shock on my face and in my voice. "You were upset with her for lying to you?" I couldn't help but laugh out loud. "You were upset because she lied. Wow! You poor thing," I said, dripping with sarcasm.

"I know, Alexandra, it is total irony. I am hurt because someone lied to me and that's all I have been doing to you for so many years."

"Oh, not only me have you been lying to but also our daughter. She has a brother that she knows nothing about and has never laid eyes on, and you're upset," I snapped.

Oliver took another deep breath. "Actually, she has laid eyes on him. The young man at the car dealership tonight, that's Robert, that's my son."

I just stood there laughing like an insane woman. "I don't even have words for you Oliver, and that's a big deal for me because I always have words."

Oliver looked down at the floor and then looked back to me with tears in his eyes, "Alex, I met with our attorney and I have filed for divorce. You will get everything we have including our house, the cabin, our investments, cars, and banking accounts. The only thing I ask for is half of the money in the savings account that you didn't know about to help take care of my kids and to live. Alexandra, I asked the lawyer not to put us on the docket until Meghan was settled in college, that way she would not see any of this taking place."

I stood there for what seemed like forever just looking at him, just staring at the man who had been the center of my life for so many years and it was far from sinking in that I was not the center of his world. "How do you plan on telling Meghan that her parents are getting divorced, Oliver? Have you thought of that yet?"

"No, Alex, I haven't. I never wanted to not be married to you Alexandra. You are the love of my life

❤ ❤ ❤ ❤ ❤ ❤ ❤ ❤ ❤ ❤ ❤ ❤ ❤

and my heart, but I can't keep putting you though this and expecting you to stay by my side."

"You know Oliver, you have taken it upon yourself to make decisions that should have been made by the two of us; affairs, kids, money, how to divide our belongings, divorce, just about everything has been your decision. You didn't have the decency to ask me about any of it," I said coldly.

"Alex are you saying you don't want a divorce?" Oliver asked with hope in his voice.

"You know, Oliver, I took my vows seriously, and when I said forever, till death do us part I meant it. I guess you had the final decision there too."

Meghan settled right in to college life, just like I knew she would. I was thrilled she had decided to attend college only a few hours from my home town. I watched the movers load all of my belongings into the truck and I stood there with memories flashing through my mind. I couldn't help but realize I had a long way to travel, not just in miles but in the healing process as well. I slid my key in the door and turned the lock for the last time, and as I walked to my car I saw Oliver sitting in his car at the curb. A part of me wanted to go talk to him, but he just smiled a small smile, waved at me and drove off. I guess throughout this marriage I believed that we had made this journey together, but now I realize that Oliver made many decisions on his own that affected both of our lives, and he decided how long his forever was.

ABOUT THE AUTHOR

 I was raised in a small town in southwest Iowa and moved to Georgia shortly after I graduated from high school. I am married with two grown children who mean the world to me and have four of the most precious grandchildren. I believe I am blessed by God to have this opportunity to publish my book, and hope that those who will read it will enjoy it.

CPSIA information can be obtained
at www.ICGtesting.com
Printed in the USA
BVHW04s1530270618
520208BV00013B/189/P

9 780999 354575